Wayfinder

A Strategy for Navigating Financial Markets

By: William P. DeCotiis

Chapter 1: Value v. Price

As mentioned in the foreword, in order to understand any topic fully one must first achieve some level of understanding of the fundamental unit that underlies the topic of interest. In the world of finance, the fundamental unit is "value". "Value" is defined as the "regard with which something is held to deserve"[1], which is a fancy way of saying value is something that has intrinsic worth. It is something useful or desirable because of its nature or inherent properties. Value is, admittedly, a very broad concept, but serves as the fundamental underpinning of economics generally. Any item of value is called an "asset".

Once an individual has acquired something of "value" (i.e. some usefulness of desirability), the usefulness and desirability of that item to the individual declines as additional units of this item are acquired. This is known as the "law of diminishing marginal utility". If I have no gold, the first unit of gold I acquire is extremely "valuable" to me. Once a threshold of my personal need is met, each unit of gold provides less enjoyment to me than the preceding unit I acquired. This is a result of our human nature and the fact that at our base we are all necessarily consumers if we desire to live. The "law of diminishing marginal utility" is easily testable for veracity by playing your favorite song on repeat. If you really love that song you might last a day or a week, but by the end of some time period, it will become less and less pleasurable to hear that song. If I were building a telephone line of copper wire, copper would be very valuable to me until I completed my

[1] https://www.dictionary.com/browse/value

telephone line and I created an adequate reserve for repairs. After that point I would place decreasing value on each additional unit of copper I acquired.

Because of the diminishing law of marginal utility, as I build up a surplus of an item of value, I become less interested in my ability to keep it (sometimes there are actually costs of storage or maintenance costs of doing so) and more interested in exchanging it for other items of value that I need to enrich my life. By way of example, if I have 2,500 egg-laying hens I can be assured that I will not starve. However, it may enrich my life greatly to trade 500 hens for one cow, such that I can have a glass of milk with my eggs.

In order to make an exchange of an item of "value" which I possess I must decide on its "price". "Price" is the amount of "value" I require in exchange for my item of value. To be clear, the "price" need not and is often not the intrinsic "value" of the item. It is a sum I designate based on my perception of its value to the individual who will be buying it from me, which is largely a result of the supply I have of my item (i.e. its value to me factoring in the diminishing marginal utility of the item), the demand for that item in the market place (i.e. how badly the individual who wants to buy it needs it relative to how badly I need to sell it) and my own personal views on the future demand/supply, relative need to the buyer and my personal attitudes toward the item. Continuing from the example above, it is quite possible that a cow is worth more than 500 hens in the general marketplace. My ability to attain the cow for a price of 500 hens is a result of a myriad of factors including but not limited to, the quality of the cow, the abundance of cows generally, the strength of my desire to acquire a cow, the desire of others to have a cow, the quality of my hens, the strength of my desire to give away my hens, the desires of others to possess hens, etc.

In short, price is what you pay for an item and the value of an item is what it is intrinsically worth.

While not a terribly conceptually difficult concepts to grasp, all finance is fundamentally based on the arbitrage between value and price. That is to say, value and price are often mismatched over time. The primary reason value and price are mismatched is because both price and value (to a lesser degree) are based on individual's subjective views of the world.

The value of an item is primarily determined by its usefulness or desirability. If an item's usefulness is replaced by a better more technologically advanced item its value diminishes for example.

Similarly, but much more dramatically, price fluctuates in accordance with the relative demand and supply of an item. At its most extreme, the underlying value of an item doesn't matter at all and the price is simply determined by the number of individuals who desire to possess an item and the amount they are willing to exchange to do so. If no one is willing to purchase an item (because there is a more technologically advanced item people would rather own, for instance) its price will diminish, quite possibly below the residual value that exists in the item's intrinsic usefulness.

This understanding of value v. price is the single most important lesson of economics. Somewhat tragically, it is also often, misunderstood by most individuals. It is in fact the underpinning of some of the most successful strategies in the history of financial markets such as "value investing", "corporate activism", consolidation of industries, etc.

receiving 20% return, I will desire more than 7% even though I do not need it for survival.

While rational decision making based on supply and demand forces certainly underpin price, the mimetic process causes dramatic swings in price as individuals perceive "value" simply because other people are purchasing an item (to be clear there has been no change or disruption to the underlying item of value other than other people seem to be valuing the item as valuable in our example). This process is as old as humankind and in fact is identifiable in ancient texts including religious texts like the Torah, the Bible and the Quran. In financial history, this process has been exhibited in countless bubbles both recently (tech bubble of the 2000s) and the past (Tulip Mania of 1637). These bubbles are often fueled by debt in which people borrow in an effort to purchase assets beyond they can afford in an effort to take part in the mimetic process (often, having fully succumbed to the mimetic process, believing that the mania will never end) (1939 stock market crash, 2009 financial crisis).

Chapter 3: Wealth Storages & the Means of Exchange

Returning to our discussion of hens and cows, it is difficult to give a proper unit value to an exchange in which goods are physically transferred. For instance, if the true value of a cow is 525.34 hens, I will most likely have to pay more or less in hens than I should for the cow (unless I am going to chop a hen into pieces, which would probably erode some of the hen's value). Similarly, it might be difficult to exchange 525.34 hens knowing that the cow will also be delivered or before I have a cow pen properly set up (said another way, it would be somewhat challenging to deliver a cow or hen in escrow). Perhaps I do not need a cow today, but would like the ability to exchange my hens today for their value so I could buy a cow in the future.[2] As can be seen from our example, a barter economy is inefficient, imprecise and difficult to administrate.

As such, people developed a "unit of exchange". That is to say, collectively, humans decided that in a society there would be some uniform item which everyone would understand to be worth a designated value which could be used in exchange for goods and services. This "unit of exchange" is called "currency". Because this currency has a designated "value" it can also serve as a storage of wealth, since all things being equal it will keep its designated "value" if I store it and do not exchange it until a later date.

---

[2] Perhaps, because I either believe the value of hens is high (a process known as "speculating") or I have an oversupply today and no room for the additional chickens (i.e. for "cost reasons" or "carrying" reasons).

As a brief caveat, it should be noted that currency (like any other item of value) is subject to the differential between price and value. Because modern currencies are so widely utilized and perceived as "safe" assets, the face "value" of a currency is typically equal to the price you have to pay to acquire such currency. However, it should be noted that in times of loss of faith in the backstop for an underlying currency (gold in gold-backed currency or the faith in the government to repay its debts with fiat currency) the price of currency can disengage from its intrinsic value causing price swings subject to the mimetic process. In the case of fiat currencies in particular, it is difficult conceptually to disengage "price" from "value" because fiat currencies have no intrinsic value, they are just paper that society agrees is worth a certain price to serve as a base unit of exchange as long as the government is in existence and able to meet its financial obligations. It is also my general belief that widespread use of fiat currency is the fundamental reason most people do not understand the difference between price and value (because economically disadvantaged individuals typically only experience wealth in the form of fiat currency and thereby believe value is equivalent to price).

Because currency in the modern age is fiat money and backed by governments, currency fluctuates relative to trade surpluses and deficits between countries. That is to say, the supply of money is carefully tailored by the government to provide efficiency in commerce between nations (just as it did with the initial barter economy, but on a larger global scale) and is manipulated by nations to account for whether they would rather be a net exporter or net importer of goods.[3] Some currency is designated as the "reserve currency" of the world, that is to say a particular country's currency is deemed safest and most commonly used around the world and as such is held in large reserves by other countries to 1) back their own currency and 2) to facility efficiency in trading with other countries. The main benefits of being a "reserve currency" are that the reserve currency mimetically is perceived as safest which adds support to its value back home and that most lenders will want their loans denominated in the reserve currency. During credit crises (when loans are defaulting) the country with the reserve currency is likely to suffer the least because they can manipulate their currency to help smooth out the damage of the credit crisis, i.e. by printing more money to counter the retraction of credit resulting from defaults (while other countries will have to suffer the result and often negative consequences to their own currencies as individuals lose faith in their home economy and their government).

To be clear, however, currency is simply a unit and means of exchange/storage of wealth, because society designates it as such and has no true "intrinsic value". Further, anything can be a "unit of exchange" or "storage of wealth" conceptually (although it will be much less efficient to trade or transfer wealth without using the social unit of exchange). As an example, if I owned 20 high rise

---

[3] Consumer economies (like the US) typically prefer a stronger currency relative to others because they are service economies and a net buyer of global goods while productive economies (like China) typically prefer a weaker currency relative to others because they are manufacturing economies and net seller of global goods. A weaker currency in your home country means you can produce a product at a lower cost and sell it to an economy where their currency is worth more than yours effectively giving you the spread in the difference of your currencies.

To be sure there are certain assets which are difficult to use for production, although I would maintain that almost any asset can be. Even currency can be lent at a price (its interest rate) with the expectation of future productive return.

I also believe this understanding is the number one factor that separates people who attain wealth from those who do not. It is far more common for individuals to acquire assets that lose value over time or to consume the full value of their assets after the initial purchase rather than to use the value of that asset to produce more income and grow in wealth. By way of example, the vast majority of individuals in the U.S. will purchase and own a home. They will live in that home and that home over time will require maintenance and additional cost. Comparatively few individuals would purchase the same house for the purpose of renting such house to another, thereby generating rental income which can be rolled into the purchase of additional rental properties. Same asset, same purchase price, two very different results.

---

[4] One hen produces 8 chicks. At adulthood the 8 chicks (now hens), produce 8 chicks each or 64 chicks.

Chapter 5: Compounding

Compounding is perhaps the most important natural phenomenon for gaining wealth through investment because exponential growth far exceeds linear growth over time. This is quite apparent graphically.

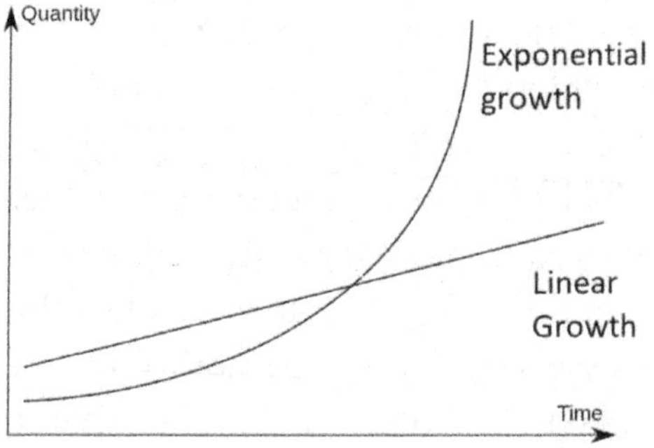

[5]

Mathematically compounding is a fairly complex mathematical phenomena, but conceptually it is a fairly simple concept. That is to say, if I have a productive asset and it produces another productive asset which I allow to produce; over time, my production will grow at an exponential growth rate rather than a linear rate.

Using our hen example, if I have a hen that produces 8 chicks and each time it produces 8 chicks I sell them, my growth in wealth will be linear. I will get the same return on my hen every time I sell the 8 chicks. That is to say, each reproductive cycle I will have only 8 chicks to sell and will receive the market price of 8 chicks in the

---

[5] https://blog.ucsusa.org/doug-boucher/world-population-growth-exponential

market when I sell them (subject to market fluctuations in perceived value and price).

If I take that same hen and keep half of the chicks it produces to produce another set of chicks each, my growth improves dramatically. My hen produces 8 chicks. I sell half of them (or 4 chicks in the first reproductive cycle) for the market price and I keep four. In the second reproductive cycle I now have 5 hens which produce 8 chicks each, which together produce 40 chicks in the next reproductive cycle (5 x 8 = 40). If I sell half of them, I now can sell 20 chicks for the market price and keep 20. In one reproductive cycle I have gone from having the ability to sell 4 chicks to the ability to sell 20 chicks (although in that first cycle I deprived myself the ability to sell the other 4 chicks, by saving those chicks and putting them to productive use, I gained the value of their production or 20 chicks which far exceeds the value I had, had I not saved those 4 chicks).

I believe this process of compounding to be the reason people say that being able to "delay gratification" is one of the pillars of wealth. If I am an impulsive person and the moment I receive something of value I desire to sell it, I deprive myself of future growth and as such the ability to compound my value in the future. The statement as you might expect however is overbroad as it doesn't take into account managing production of productive assets or realization of value overtime (there is no need for instance to starve oneself to death when a chicken would keep one alive), but generally is true.[6]

---

[6] As an example, many people who are high salary individuals tend to consume as much as they receive in income or more than they receive in income (which they do by taking on debt borrowing from the their

To be sure there is a balance to be struck, one must consume to live and there is no harm in enjoying one's production (I myself sold half of my chicks in the first reproductive cycle), however it is harmful to consume all of which one's assets produce, because it stymies future growth, which compounds with time (which I believe is the crux of the old adage).

Interestingly, compounding is, more than anything, a gift from the natural order in that productive things tend to produce (through reproduction) productive things of their same kind (a marvel of the natural world). It is also, mathematically, one of the single most important aspect to growing wealthy. That is to say, one's rate of return, (i.e. the rate at which our hen produced chicks), the amount of time one has to allow productive assets to compound, the amount of productive assets one begins with, the cost of maintaining one's productive assets and one's rate of consumption (i.e. the variables in the mathematical equation of compounding) are the primary determinants of whether one grows in wealth.

These eight levers: 1) rate of return, 2) the certainty of such return, 3) time, 4) the amount capital available to invest, 5) the amount of productive assets needed for consumption, 6) the amount of productive assets which can be reinvested, 7) the cost of maintaining the invested assets and 8) the risk of loss of invested capital; are the pillars of finance and wealth generally and the determinants/variables for growing in wealth. As a general rule, the higher your rate of return, the longer the time period, the more capital

---

future selves) and as such live their entire life without any financial independence despite having the means to do so, for no other reason than they lack self-control.

as the living cells run out of food and begin to receive chemical signals from dying cells around them that they should die also (through a process called apoptosis).

Graphically this is why growth charts tend to take on an S-curve (Ch. 4 Fig. 1) if the growth rate can be maintained by adding enough input to sustain the growth level that was achieved or a death chart (Ch.4 Fig. 2) if that growth can't be maintained.

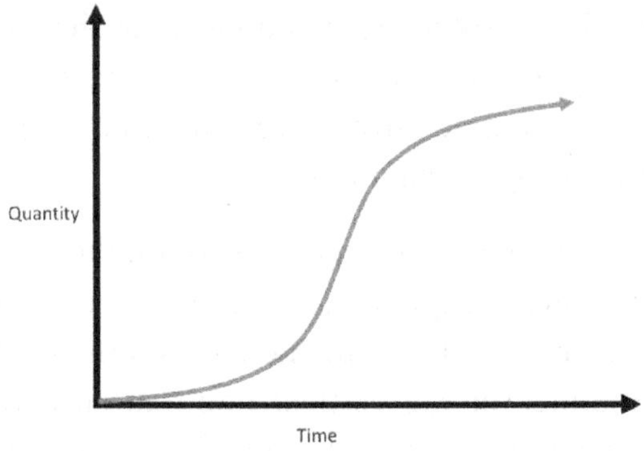

Chapter 4, Figure 1.

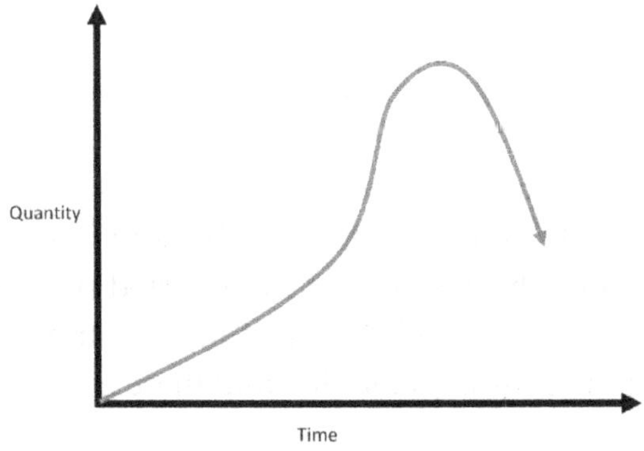

Chapter 4, Figure 2.

In finance this same process observed in biology with cellular growth and death occurs, although it is less understood.[8] Effectively financial growth occurs, until it reaches an unsustainable point, at which point it dies (or sells off) to a level that is more sustainable.[9] This "death" continues until there is a sustainable "food source" at which point, price stabilizes and begins to grow again until it reaches another unstable level.

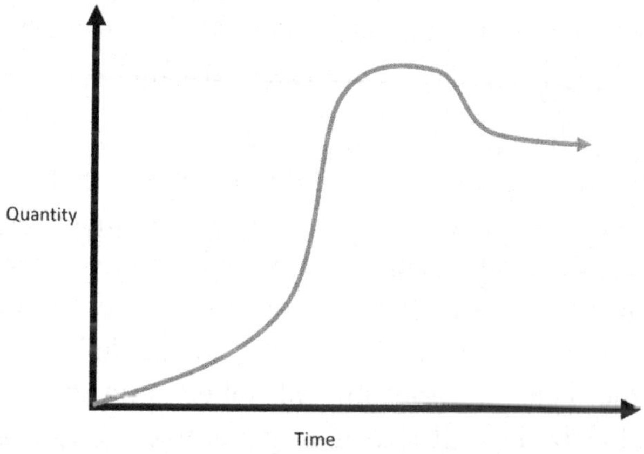

By way of example in the finance world, the "death" phase will occur for a business (really any business product line) when such business runs out of customers and as such is unable to create new sustainable user or consumer growth. At this point growth will flat line perhaps even decrease as new competitors enter the market or try to take market share. For a particularly successful or innovative company this may not occur until all of the

[8] This is the fundamental concept behind "mean reversion", which will be discussed further in Chapter 18.

[9] Because the sustainable level of growth is most likely to be the "average growth rate" of a financial asset, this will look like a "return to the mean".

consumers on the planet are captured at which point the company will be a monopoly. While extremely valuable at this point, growth will stall and future growth will require a price hike to enjoy future cash flow growth. The business will be able to hike price until consumers begin to leave, which further depresses growth, or if the business is a monopoly, consumers will not be able to leave because there is no place else to go, but at this point, governments usually step in to prevent price hiking which is understood historically to be the next step after consumer or user growth stalls to increase cash flow growth.

While perhaps not immediately clear, it is worth noting that the behavior of exhibited in our cell example is true for any productive asset. The cells themselves are a productive asset in that they produce more of themselves which can in turn produce more of themselves, until they run out of room or food. As such, the modeling that is true for the cells is true for all other productive assets[10]. Whether by natural causes or government intervention, all productive assets have a life cycle just like the cells in the lab.

---

[10] That is to say, exponential growth modeling which is itself built on layered linear growth modeling.

Chapter 6: Equity v. Debt

All assets can be purchased in one of two ways: with ownership, i.e. exchanging something you own (or something individuals who you convince to buy the asset alongside you own) of value for ownership in the new asset (equity) or by borrowing from someone else to buy said asset with the promise to pay back the money at a certain rate (debt). All assets are necessarily owned by either equity or debt (for large assets like corporations typically both) if they are purchased.

This fundamental truth is the basis for the "balance sheet" in financial accounting in which the total equity and total debt of a company must mathematically equal the total assets of the corporation. It is also why the fundamental metric for evaluating any business is its "equity value". That is to say, its assets (minus intangible assets like goodwill) minus debt. The "equity value" is the total value of the assets owned by the equity holders. As such it also represents the amount of money left over from selling assets in a liquidation or bankruptcy to satisfy outstanding debts.

Colloquially, for an asset purchased with both debt and equity, the equity holders are considered the "owners" of the asset (since they have the ability to control and direct the asset) and the debt holders are considered "creditors" of the asset (since they have a claim to underlying assets if the principal of their investment is not returned along with interest on the borrowed money). Generally speaking, however, both have a "property claim" to the asset.

In the case of debt, to secure the fact that the borrower will repay the amount of money borrowed, a lender will typically require "collateral". "Collateral" is a legally binding agreement (typically given the power of "property rights") that a lender can take some portion of an asset that has residual value if the borrower fails to pay back the money borrowed. In most cases the "collateral" will be a legally binding agreement to take all or a portion of the asset that was purchased with the borrowed money. (As will be discussed further below some loans are "unsecured" but because of the additional risk will typically be more expensive, i.e. have a much higher interest rate).

To be clear, permitting an asset to be owned with debt gives the equity holders additional purchasing power, typically referred to as "leverage" (i.e. the ability to purchase something they couldn't with their own money), but at the cost of paying the money back over time (typically, out of future earnings from the equity's ownership). For a productive asset, debt can be boost returns (as discussed further below) by pocketing the spread between the productivity of the asset against the cost of the borrowed money. For a non- or low-productive asset taking on a large amount of debt can be devasting to the asset and the equity holders.

as there are a variety of ways to evaluate return factoring time decay and the like) we see that we can achieve 8.14% growth annually (or "per annum") in our example. Overtime, if we can take that income that is produced (that 8.14%) and reinvest it (let's assume for ease into the same investment or another investment that produces the same return) that 8.14% will result in the growth of our capital exponentially at a 8.14% growth rate. At an 8.14% rate of return we will receive roughly the same amount of money in income as our initial investment in approximately 9 years.

The question of course is whether that growth rate is "good". Whether or not our growth rate is "good" is primarily determined by 1) whether you can get a better growth rate from an asset of the same level of risk (i.e. the risk you won't get any return or will lose your purchase price), i.e. comparison to other similar assets, 2) the amount of risk you are willing to take (i.e. whether you are willing to take a greater chance of losing your money for a better growth rate), 3) how much income you need to produce for consumption and production purposes and 4) your time horizon (i.e. how long you want to be invested in a particular asset / how long you intend to invest for generally).

To be clear, this analysis works for any investment you want to evaluate. That is to say any productive asset can be viewed through this lens. The first step is to determine what income the asset produces. The income is then compared to the purchase price to identify a growth rate. The growth rate is calculated over a designated a time horizon for which one desires to invest and compared against the risk of loss over such time horizon.

This is true for whether you are investing in a chicken farm, your veterinarians' business, a sandwich shop, a golf course or a Fortune 500 company. It is also true for your income from your job. You can quite effectively, calculate your income, your future likely salary increases, and determine the value of working for your productive working life, to determine how much money you will make and at what rate of return.

If you have no productive assets other than yourself, you will likely have to work to get a lump sum of productive asset enough to work for you, at least initially. To be sure however, the goal should be to have your money do your work for you and not to work forever until you die (unless you really love what you do). To be sure, the earlier you are able to do this, the more wealthy you will become. [11]

---

[11] This desire to be wealthy is also a significant contributing factor to bull and bear markets. People typically want as much money as possible as soon as possible, so they take on more and more risk (especially during good times).

The most greedy among us typically use leverage to do this, and as such put their assets at additional risk during negative times. During good times, people tend to discount risks that they should otherwise consider and when a downturn strikes they lose more than they anticipated which can have a terrible impact on return depending on the loss suffered in addition to putting their principal at risk.

Mimetically people will tend to take the risks other people are taking (perceiving safety in being part of the crowd) and as such will suffer even greater loss when everyone gets scared of losing their value at the same time. Interestingly the number one snake oil sales pitch, by asset managers and investment bankers is that you can get additional return without corresponding risk. As we will see shortly, that is almost entirely untrue in all cases with the exception of skillful diversification, skilled market timing/understanding of cycles or expert hedging. Almost all asset managers are selling one of these three things (usually more than one) as experts in doing so. Almost all asset

Because humans have a designated life span (within a range), for you to enjoy the benefit of your money working for you, the sooner you can begin having productive assets work for you the better and the more you can control your consumption until you have enough productive assets the better[12]. Although philosophically that will also be a choice between how well you want to live and at what stage of your life you would like to live it (depending on the amount of investment capital you have to start with).

---

managers are also terrible at these things.

It is also worth noting that people perceive safety in crowds because of the mimetic process. If something works for someone else, then it should work for us as the logic goes. However, as you might expect this is much too simple and doesn't account for the myriad of variables affecting a decision. Just because everyone else has walked across a bridge and it hasn't fallen down doesn't mean that when you walk across it, it won't crack and break. You would be much safer to evaluate the bridge's safety features, max capacity load, weather conditions etc., but that is all terribly complicated so humans simplify risk analysis to shrugging one's shoulder and saying "I don't know seems to have worked for them". To be sure for the most part that will work, the bridge is probably fine if 10,000 people have walked across it, the danger is when it doesn't and you are unprepared for the negative consequences of not evaluating risk for yourself.

[12] Although you could if you are so inclined, forward thinking and benevolent set up future generations of your family for great wealth by planting the seed of productive assets today for their benefit.

Ratios

	Monthly	Yearly
Debt Service Coverage Ratio	2.91	2.91
Cap Rate (Purchase Price)	0.24%	2.93%
Net Cash Flow Percentage	18.49%	18.49%
Cash on Cash Return	1.22%	14.65%

Taking our cash flow example from Chapter 5, an asset with a purchase price of $100,000 and cash flow of $2,929.23 may be an attractive cash on cash return of 8.14%, but is of little use to you if you don't have $100,000 to purchase it with in the first place. Assuming we don't have $100,000 available as capital for investment, we have two main options, 1) source capital or "fundraise" by asking other people to buy the asset along with us and/or 2) ask to borrow some money to purchase it. If we "fundraise", the downside is those individuals who buy in with us will be partial owners and as such will be able to control or direct use of the asset and will share in any profits it receives (typically proportionately to how much of the purchase price they contributed). If we borrow money, we don't have to share control or profits (other than a security interest, which will permit the lender to step in and exhibit control if we fail to pay back their money aka "default" or become "insolvent" or "bankrupt"), but we do need to pay back the money at whatever the price of borrowing the money was (that is to say the interest rate and any upfront fees). Because we neither have to share control or profits when we borrow money, borrowing money is considered a "cheaper" form of capital for purchasing an asset than giving away equity because we don't have to give up any portion of the purchased asset (assuming that the borrowed cost of money doesn't exceed cash flow from the asset). Thus, the inherent benefit of debt, is that it allows one to borrow money to buy something one couldn't otherwise own without giving up control or profit.

Conceptually, taking on debt can also be viewed as extending the purchase price of an asset over time. For instance, although you may not have $100,000 today, you may have a job that produces $50,000 per year, so in two years you may have $100,000. Using leverage allows you to purchase the asset today, even though you don't have the money today, by permitting you to pay back the $100,000 over time secured by your income. This is how most people in the United States of America purchase a home. Few people have the upfront cash to purchase their home, but most middle-class Americans have a job where they can afford to pay back the cost of their home over fifteen to thirty years based on their income. This is also why the mortgage process is so extensive, since a bank will want to ensure that you have sufficient income over time to pay back the money they gave you today to purchase your home.

However, as we already discussed the home you live in is not a productive asset (which is in fact why we have to rely on you your own income to pay it back), because the house is not used to produce any value and will in fact have additional maintenance costs over time. Although it might "appreciate in value" as time goes on, despite what many people would tell you, the home you live in is not a productive asset (and in my view not an investment). This is why it can be quite dangerous to take on too many personal loans, since if you lose your job or something bad happens to you the promise of that future cash flow from your income may diminish and when that occurs it becomes very difficult to ever pay the money back depending on how much you borrowed.

This quite tragically is true of student loans. Many people looking to pay for college they couldn't afford took out loans, with the only productive asset underlying them being the future cash flow derived from their income in their future career. Even more tragically and because most people don't understand leverage properly, they took out more debt than their future career's expected income could support. In real numbers, it is not uncommon for someone to have $250,000 in student loan debt and a career that produces only $50,000 annually. After adding in living expenses and other costs, someone in this financial situation may never be able to pay back their loans or live well. Personal loans generally run this risk and should be kept as minimal as possible, where possible since they are not supported by a productive asset or a scalable asset (since there is only and will only be one of you and your income is unlikely to grow exponentially).

Conversely, leverage on a productive asset can vastly improve one's rate of return. Going back to our cash flow example, we can see that our $100,000 asset produces $15,840.00 per year. After we subtract out the costs it takes to maintain the asset it still produces $8,380.00 per year. We didn't have $100,000 upfront (we only had $20,000), so we borrowed the remaining $80,000 at a cost of 5.5% compounded monthly or $5,450.77 per year. Because our asset after maintenance costs produces 8,380.00 per year and our loan cost is $5,450.88 per year, our productive asset pays off the $80,000 portion of the purchase price using the income it generates itself and we receive the surplus of $2929.23 per year as profit until the loan is paid off.

If the asset produces its income steadily for the life of the loan, we will have acquired the asset using its own "future cash flow" that is to say, the borrowed money was paid off over time by the cash flow the productive asset produced over time. Additionally because while it was paying itself off, we still received the excess profit our "Cash on Cash" return was dramatically increased from 8.14% to 14.65% since we spent only 20% of the purchased price but still enjoyed 18.49% of the Net Cash Flow annually. In terms of years, we will now receive the entire value of our investment after 6 years as opposed to 8 years. This is the primary value of leverage, it allows you to acquire assets with minimal equity capital thereby increasing cash on cash return and allowing a productive asset to bear the weight of the cost of the borrowed capital.

The contrast here is quite dramatic. Taking on a personal loan means that I have to sacrifice my future income until it is paid off, but leveraging a productive asset means the productive assets sacrifices a portion of its future income, while providing me with residual profit.

As you might intuit, this is a very attractive trade in that I can spend less to purchase more than I can afford and the asset I buy will pay itself off, while still giving me a return on my money superior to the rate of return had I bought the asset in its entirety on day one.

In case it is not clear, the reason for this is a result of the interplay between price and income. That is to say, the purchase price relative to the income that asset

constant tension between the interests of equity and lenders which is fundamentally based on the risk-limiting benefits to equity of acquiring an asset with leverage in a bankruptcy remote structure.

It is also worth noting that we added a key ratio, the "Debt Service Coverage Ratio" or "DSCR", in our model, which represents the amount of cash flow the asset produces to cover its loan payment. In our example above, the cash flow is equal to 2.1 times the loan payment and is therefore considered fairly safe. Depending on how much cash flow covers the loan payment (or the DSCR) and the certainty of the future cash flow, investment bankers will evaluate risk and consider different prices on their loans (i.e. different interest rates) and different collateral requirements.

Leverage, Modern Financial Markets, and the Securitization Chain

Interestingly, this rather simple concept of cash flow when combined with leverage makes up the majority of financial evaluation in investment banking and "private equity" which for purposes of this book we will describe as purchasing a private enterprise or asset for the sake of cash flow returns.

Private equity has been quite successful since the 1980s because over that time period the cost of a loan (that is interest rate costs) have been far lower than investment returns on most assets and has made acquiring on leverage extremely attractive and lucrative. Because of the added benefit of bankruptcy remoteness, asset managers have figured out that they can set up a management entity, which selects investments for purchase, and acquire a fee based on purchased asset performance (typically a percentage of return) without outlaying any capital of their own (or limited capital), instead sourcing "equity" capital from pension funds, insurance premiums and other financial institutions which at their heart aggregate the collective wealth of the masses. This equity capital can then be leveraged to buy a wide variety of productive assets with attractive return. Because of the use of leverage, the equity used is a relatively small portion of the assets purchased and deemed "under management" of the manager and the manager enjoys the fee and return associated with performance of this larger pool of assets.

Additionally because of bankruptcy remoteness, when those assets fail to perform, the lenders and the equity of those whom they raised capital from will suffer, but the manager will remain bankruptcy remote (and funds will remain remote from one another, each in their own separate silo despite being managed by the same manager). As such this creates a significant moral hazard on the part of the manager to take on more and more risk to generate increased returns (as well as much leverage as a lender will permit them to have), since the manager shares in the upside, but has no skin (or limited skin) in the game on the downside. Such a situation creates significant moral hazard since managers get rich risking other people's money on leverage for their own personal gain.

For the sake of not solely singling out private equity, which on the whole is a very effective model for generating return (depending on your personal views on the moral hazard aspect[14]), I should mention that hedge funds

---

[14] I would note, just for interest, that views on the moral hazard of this model tend to vary depending on which side of the model one is on,

employ largely the same leverage strategy albeit in public markets with public stocks as do a variety of holding

---

the overall market conditions and the relative outrage/sympathetic nature of those impacted disproportionately. As an example, in the 2009 crisis, the industry impacted most disproportionately was the real estate industry, which resulted in many individuals losing their homes. The 2009 crisis, also severely impacted, the financial industry and banking (almost all crises do, since almost all industries in crisis are over-leveraged). During this crisis, the U.S. financial industry was particularly vulnerable because it is extremely concentrated as a result of certain banking rules and regulations, most notably the repeal of the Glass-Steagall Act, which removed a structural safeguard against the financial sector that was put in place after the Great Depression. When the financial industry breaks down, banks stop extending credit, which has the effect of reducing monetary supply further exacerbating falling asset prices. To curtail a nationwide crisis, since the average homeowner is a sympathetic individual from a policy standpoint, the U.S. government used taxpayer money to re-capitalize most of the large financial institutions, whose greed and securitization structure resulted in the toxic assets which caused the crisis. This use of taxpayer money to "bail-out" greedy (and typically) rich Wall Street types who caused the problem to begin with caused significant political upheaval and the income inequality which resulted from providing artificial liquidity to financial assets continues to plague society and influence political discussions to this day. In the next crisis, pension funds and insurance companies are likely to be significantly exposed and disproportionately impacted as a result of their heavy investment in private equity, private credit and corporate debt generally (at a time when obligations on these various pensions and insurance companies are likely to be exacerbated by an aging population). As you might surmise, pension funds and insurance companies are particularly sympathetic because the underlying individual who will be hurt is the ordinary, aging American, who worked their whole life with the expectation that these institutions would care for them in retirement. As such, as a matter of social policy, it seems likely another taxpayer bail-out will be sought (the cynic might even say, many managers are betting that the sympathetic nature of the pension recipient is so severe that a bail-out can be reasonably expected).

companies, insurance companies and various other investment companies. I should also note that in addition to leverage from a traditional loan, there are numerous ways to receive lent money through derivatives contracts, letters of credit, leveraged loans, and other structured products.

It is also worth mentioning that in modern times, lending has taken a form not seen historically. That is to say, in the 2000s bankers developed a technique known as the "securitization chain".

The securitization chain is a process by which lenders realized that rather than take on the risk of a loan on a productive asset, such loan could be packaged into financial instruments and sold. Effectively and quite intelligently, bankers realized that a loan was itself a productive asset (that is to say it is cash lent at a cost which then creates the promise of future cash flow payments over time). Because a loan produces income, the loan itself could be packaged into bankruptcy remote vehicles and sold as smaller units as "securities" in the debt markets (for ease it is fine to think of loans being packaged into bonds which are then sold). These debt securities are then marketed as "productive assets" which themselves can be put into bankruptcy remote vehicles and purchased at a price using leverage. The end result of this securitization chain is that the lender who evaluates the initial loan never bears the risk of the loan (the originator), but rather sells that risk to investors who purchase the asset and thereafter are entitled to future cash flow in proportion to the amount of debt purchased and thereby bear a portion of the risk of the loan (in proportion to their purchase).

mismanagement). When price to book is less than 1 a company becomes a target for a hostile takeover, since one can effectively purchase the company and sell of its assets for salvage value at a profit (since the net assets are more valuable than the company as a whole), although in modern times due to legal constructs like poison pills and the like, hostile takeovers are more difficult.

Once the inherent value of an asset can be arrived at, it is important to compare said value to the purchase price being asked. Often the price of an asset will have a premium over the mathematical value of the asset, because of "goodwill" (brand names deemed valuable, customer relationships and other intangibles), expectations of earnings growth beyond what is modeled, supply or demand constraints or surpluses, in the case of real estate desirable or unique locations, in addition to a myriad of other factors. Similarly, a distressed asset, can have a price discounted below the mathematical value of an asset, because of some negative event impacting the value, uncertainty of future cash flow, perceived market risk or a myriad of other factors. It is also important to note that some assets have no productive value, but are simply consumable. These assets, known as "commodities", are priced solely based on supply and demand (and inflation) as they have no ability to produce cash flow inherently.

From our cash flow example before, if we have an asset with Net Cash Flow of $8,380 and a useful life of 10 years, the approximate value of the asset is $83,800 (ignoring any salvage value the asset has assuming it is a real asset and the cost of capital overtime). At a purchase price of $100,000 we paid a premium of $16,200 to acquire the asset which could have been a result of supply and demand, goodwill, an expectation of future cash flow growth or a host of other factors affecting price.

It should be noted that while valuation itself has a component of speculation (that is the discount or premium accounting for future growth or decline), price layers on an additional layer of factors which are far more speculative than simply earnings and is subject to mimetic forces to a great extent. Speculation often leads to large mimetic cycles which result in bubbles and troughs. We will discuss price fluctuations and how to account for trends in price more thoroughly in Chapter 18.

Because unchecked inflation and deflation can completely destroy a currency's value and thereby destabilize the government and society itself, inflation and deflation is controlled (or "stabilized") by manipulating the risk-free rate (referred to as the "treasury rate" in the U.S.). This is primarily done by the Federal Reserve in the U.S. by adjusting the "federal funds target rate" (which is, generally speaking, the deposit rate the Federal Reserve charges to hold money of large institutions, and is generally seen as the rate all other rates are essentially compared against in the U.S.) to account for inflation and deflationary forces. The idea is to smooth the extremes of the market forces to keep one's currency stable.[18]

As you might imagine, however, when individuals and governments figure out they can manipulate something to cause a result they begin to do so and as time has gone on governments have become keenly aware that by manipulating the "treasury rate" and thereby manipulating the risk-free rate they can encourage or discourage all kinds of investment behavior, since all other rates of return are inherently mathematically calculated with a risk premium relative to the risk free rate of return.

---

supply, which is "inflationary" (i.e. the supply of money increases). So eventually, naturally, continual lending will result in an increase in the monetary supply which will cause inflation. Inflation will continue until lenders stop lending because of inflationary forces, which is "deflationary", at which point, the decrease in lenders decreases the monetary supply.

[18] Theoretically, the Federal Reserve is tasked with maintaining a "neutral rate", i.e. the equilibrium rate at which monetary policy is neither contracting or expanding, inflation is stable and the employment is stable.

Poor management of the "treasury rate" can cause mis-pricing in the risk-free rate relative to natural market forces and can cause "poor market behavior". That is to say, it can encourage lending when people shouldn't be lending and it can discourage lending when lending is needed. For the most part (as we will discuss shortly) since the U.S. (and most modern economies generally) are comfortable carrying a heavy debt load at all times, extending additional credit is considered positive (since it juices the return and encourages growth as we saw earlier) and governments prefer lenders to be skewed toward lending.

To accomplish this, governments tend to keep the risk-free rate as low as possible (i.e. without stoking inflation), to encourage investors to seek a better rate of return elsewhere albeit at a greater risk (unless forced to raise rates to account for inflation and maintain a supply of credit). Lowering the risk-free rate is also very effective tool to re-encourage lending when credit is drying up (that is to say, if your economy has entered a recession and is contracting and people are not lending because they are fearful, you can effectively give your economy a shot in the arm, by reducing your risk-free rate so low that it is unattractive to hold cash and people begin lending back into risk).[19]

The danger of this of course, is that if sustainable growth isn't produced in the immediately proceeding period to generate real returns, keeping the risk-free rate low induces debt bubbles as growth becomes almost

[19] History tends to indicate that it takes an approximate 400 basis point reduction in the risk-free rate to counteract a deflationary recession.

entirely field by increasing amounts of debt. Politically it is also incredibly difficult to get people behind raising rates, because the immediate effect of raising rates is some de-leveraging (since the increased interest expense eats into the return expected by the equity holders/risk takers purchasing risky assets) which typically causes a short-term contraction provided sustainable growth is sufficient to pick up the slack and keep growth moving forward (if growth was unsustainable, it can cause a recession). As a result, politicians prefer to error on the side of keeping rates as low as possible for as long as possible, because no one wants to accidently cause a recession and as such, no one addresses the problem of mountains of debt on high risk assets, until those assets stop performing (or until inflation must be addressed). When those assets stop performing, defaults on debt occur, which result in credit contraction (lenders won't lend additional money into a non-paying asset) and a deleveraging occurs in an uncontrolled fashion (i.e. a crash).

This has been true since the dawn of time. Government entities have manipulated the extension of credit for societal purposes since the first civilizations. In fact, debt write-downs and forgiveness have been performed for societal benefits dating back to ancient Mesopotamia.[20] King Hammurabi of Babylon is believed to have forgiven all citizen debts owed to the government in 1792 BC in ancient Babylon (to much jubilation and fanfare).[21] In Jewish Mosaic Law, debts were cancelled every seventh Sabbath year and every 49th year was a

---

[20] https://www.telegraph.co.uk/finance/economics/11383374/The-biggest-debt-write-offs-in-the-history-of-the-world.html
[21] Id.

"Year of Jubilee" which resulted in the freedom of all debts and servitude.[22]

Debt by its nature creates excess because you borrow from someone else to purchase what you cannot afford today, gambling that you will produce enough in the future to return the money you borrowed. When that future date of repayment comes, there are two potential outcomes: 1) the debtor pays the creditor what is owed or 2) the debtor defaults on payment and the creditor seeks recourse against the debtor for failing on their promise.

In the modern age, the fear of recourse from a creditor to the defaulting debtor is diminished by bankruptcy remoteness (and securitization). That is to say, generally speaking, as an equity holder you do not need to care about losing someone else's money after you have received your return (as we saw earlier), since the only recourse will be to the asset itself and not other assets you might possess. However, you may still be incentivized to act responsibly (and not lose your creditor's money), because you may want to keep the productive asset you leveraged for the purpose of receiving future returns and not have the lender seize it (assuming it is a productive asset with productive life remaining).

Conversely, if you properly know how to use a bankruptcy remote structure, have succeeded in raising other's equity capital to purchase productive assets, and receive a fee based on the performance of those assets "under management", you as the "asset manager" (and

---

[22] Id. Interestingly these seven year and forty-nine year time horizons of the Old Testament, still fairly accurately reflect the estimated length of modern short-term and long-term debt cycles.

Additionally, artificially low rates have the effect of degrading the value of the government's currency overtime. That is to say, if rates are artificially low, borrowers are incentivized to borrow, which has the effect of increasing the monetary supply (since borrowers are borrowing from their future selves and placing that money in the marketplace). If the monetary supply increases enough, inflation will result which has the effect of diminishing the value of the government's currency. Thus, leaving the government interest rate artificially low will erode the government's purchasing power overtime.

In situations such as these, governments tend to borrow increasingly to make up for short-falls in their spending and the general lack of purchasing power of the money they do have. This leads to what's called a "fiscal deficit", that is to say the growth in debt (and the costs of servicing the government's debt) begins to exceed revenue growth, which is the first sign of any business (let alone a government) headed for insolvency (as we say earlier cash flow growth should always exceed debt servicing requirements in order for a productive asset to produce and not be "insolvent or "underwater"). When government's fail to reign in their spending and costs in the face of mounting debt, they are forced to 1) raise additional revenue (i.e. increase taxes on its citizens, which tends to cause an economic slow-down perpetuating the problem rather than solving it and also tends to disadvantage those who responsibly managed themselves since they have to provide the same tax revenues as those who over-extended themselves, or increase GDP such that additional tax

---

reducing borrowing costs (i.e. lowering interest rates) to provide market liquidity and induce investment in risk-assets.

revenue is collected from such additional production), 2) cut spending programs and costs (which is unpopular and typically unfairly damages the already disadvantaged which causes political instability) or 3) increase the supply of money by printing more money (a form of "refinancing" if you will, but which has an inflationary affect since there is now more money for every good that is available, further devaluing the currency; which at its worst, called "hyper-inflation", can cause a loss of faith in the government's currency and typically creates social instability).[26]

One and two above are mathematical options which result from our equation for net cash flow in Chapter 7. If you have taken on too much debt such that you have negative cash flow, your asset will either fail and you will default, or you can increase revenue or cut operating costs (if you can). Mathematically those are the only levers available, neither of which is particularly politically popular on a national scale.[27]

The third option, is unique to governments because they have the ability to control the unit of exchange as a social function (and governments have unmoored currency from any hard asset because doing so allows them to manipulate currency in this way for social reasons). By way of quick example, if a currency is tied to gold or another physical asset (or supply is finite as in Bitcoin™) and the costs of goods rises dramatically relative to people's faith in the currency (i.e. inflation), the currency

---

[26] Hyperinflation spirals almost always result from government budget deficits financed by money printing. Inflation is generally combatted by raising borrowing costs (i.e. interest rates).

[27] Of these options, an increase in GDP is the most beneficial, but is difficult to produce sustainably in most cases.

"growth stocks" and slower growing but more consistent cash flow generators are considered "value stocks".

The Continuum of Risk Assets

As mentioned earlier in this chapter, after the risk-free rate of return there are a variety of assets of increasing risk, which form a "continuum of risk assets". This once again is not an exhaustive list but a structure in which various assets fit quite readily that can be used as a guide for understanding what risk you are taking for the relative expected return. To be sure there are always price mismatches and price doesn't always properly reflect risk on an individual security (when that is in your favor you should buy them and when it is not you should avoid them). In any case, on a law of large numbers basis this structure will generally be true for securities of similar type.

<u>The Risk Free-Rate and Government Debt</u>

As a starting point we begin with the risk-free rate. The risk-free rate is a rate at which you receive return with no investment risk and complete certainty of cash flow income. This is typically government debt of the most stable debt instrument the most stable government provides. In the case of the U.S. this is the U.S. T-Bill. For most of the European Union this is the German Bund.

As you might expect, however, various other governments which are less stable also seek to borrow money and as such there is a continuum of risk based on the perceived financial stability of various government entities. This is true globally from country to country and is also true within a country.

With regard to various government entities within a country, in the U.S. there is a fractal of government overlaying the land we call the United States of America. We have the Federal Government on a national scale, then state governments, then county governments and then municipal governments. Each of these governmental units seek debt financing and correspondingly pay a return on such debt at increasing rates corresponding with their relative risk (as you might expect as you get smaller you get more risky). It is notable that to induce municipal government lending for social reasons, the Federal Government exempts such income from taxes which makes what would often otherwise be an unattractive rate of return more attractive to investors.

Second, debt instruments (including debt instruments backed by a country) require a risk premium based on the length of time money will be lent to entice investors to lend for such time period. This is referred to as the "duration" risk (or time risk) and therefore the risk-free rate of a government will increase if that same instrument is for longer periods of time (i.e. the interest rate should increase across bonds with lengths of 3-months, 10-years and 30 years respectfully).

With regard to duration, the longer money is lent, the more risky the investment is considered. This is largely true, because of the fact that the longer money is out in the market, the more things that can potentially happen in the interim which could change your initial investment decision.[30] Thus, the longer currency is exposed to market

[30] By way of analogy, the ship is safest on the dry-dock, but the ship also isn't doing anything productive. The longer the ship is in the ocean the more potential bad things that can happen to the ship.

forces the more risky it is considered. As such, a longer duration instrument (like a 10-year or 30-year treasury note) will require a risk premium to compensate investors for that risk beyond the risk-free rate (which is typically a short duration instrument). The exception to this is situations in which bond investors expect an economically detrimental event. In such case, bond investors flock to "safety" and buy so many risk-free rate assets of longer duration that it actually drives the price up beyond the cost of shorter duration risk-free assets. This is called "yield inversion" and is a hallmark pre-recession signal. Generally speaking though, additional duration means additional risk and requires additional return for investors to take on such risk, even if backed by the same entity as the risk-free rate.

I would also note that while I have listed government debt separately for purposes of this analysis because it differs in nature from corporate and other more traditional forms of debt, it is important to note that government debt is not strictly part of the "risk-free" asset continuum as government debt can be spread across "risk-free", "investment grade", and "high-yield" depending on its relative risk.

Investment Grade Debt

Investment Grade Debt is debt that is less safe than the risk-free rate, but is considered safe enough based on certain standards of cash flow, debt service reserve ratios, and underlying asset performance stability that society (via

---

Short journeys of the ship in and around the harbor and ending with said ship sitting comfortably on the dry-dock are from a probability perspective less likely to cause harm then a similarly situated ship that is left out in the ocean for longer periods.

government regulation) has decided that we are comfortable permitting systemically important financial institutions to invest in them. These include debt on large corporations with a long track record of earnings performance, infrastructure that we perceive as producing sustainable cash flow relative to its debt load for long periods of time, utilities, etc.

Within Investment Grade Debt there is a continuum of risk labeled by "nationally recognized statistical rating organizations" or "NRSROs" with various metrics (ranging from AAA to BBB). It is important to note, however, that as exhibited in the 2009 Financial Crisis, NRSROs are subject to manipulation and don't fully account for risk often because they are incentivized not to in good times in exchange for additional fees from organizations (mainly investment banks or conduits of investment banks) who issue or underwrite the issuance of debt.[31]

High Yield or Junk Debt

Debt that has a rating below BBB is considered "speculative" or "junk". That is to say, such debt is vulnerable to default in the event of cash flow stress. In recent times, issuers have tried to rebrand this type of debt

---

[31] For their part, most investment professionals and investment bankers tend to lend almost no credence to NRSRO ratings in making risk and investment decisions, viewing these ratings instead as regulatory compliance and marketing. It is further, not uncommon, for an investment grade asset to experience a negative event and following the negative event to be suddenly downgraded to "junk status". Thus, an NRSROs rating has almost no strategic value for evaluating individual investment risk (since such ratings are inherently backward looking) other than as a general filter of investments meeting certain criteria at a given time (in addition to their regulatory compliance and marketing functions).

be offered to potential lenders/investors to induce them to give you the money to purchase the productive asset. The main forms of capital one can raise to make a purchase (or finance ongoing asset production) are as follows:

Senior secured debt

Senior secured debt is considered highest in priority and therefore safest in the capital structure. That is to say, senior secured debt receives the lowest return, but is entitled to receive any value in the company first before all other creditors and equity in the event of a liquidation or insolvency. To provide additional security, senior secured debt also has a contractual right to foreclose on underlying assets (typically the ability to foreclose can occur outside of bankruptcy for the sake of expedience but will also be respected in/after a bankruptcy proceeding has been initiated). Typically, this contractual right, is "perfected" through a recordation process to give the creditor the force of a "property right" in the underlying asset.

Senior unsecured debt

Senior unsecured debt has the same priority of payment as senior secured debt, but has no rights to collateral.

Junior secured debt

Junior secured debt is considered "subordinated", in that it is paid only after the senior debt (and is therefore "subordinate" to that debt), but contains a right to collateral in the event of liquidation (although its claim in such collateral is subordinated to any senior secured debt). If "junior secured debt" is secured against the same assets as other higher priority debt (like senior secured debt), it is considered a “second lien loan” since the lien on the collateral is second in priority (and therefore second in liquidation) to the first lien loan (i.e. the senior secured debt).

Junior unsecured debt

Junior unsecured debt has the same priority of payment as junior secured debt, but has no rights to collateral.

Mezzanine debt and convertible debt

Mezzanine debt is a form of high interest rate debt that has no access to collateral and is paid out only after all other debt is paid. However, it often contains a “kicker” typically in the form of warrants that convert to equity at a later time. Because of the high interest rate and the nature of the loans (which include payment-in-kind interest, kickers and other equity like incentives) such debt is considered to give “equity-like” return although it looks like debt on its face (i.e. is “structured as debt”). The primary benefit to a mezzanine lender is that income interest is tax deductible (although practically you get an equity-like return).

More generally, convertible debt (including but not limited to mezzanine debt), is debt (like warrants) that can be converted to equity at a later time.

Preferred Equity

Preferred equity is equity which entitles the holder to cash flow prior to common equity but no voting rights.

Common Equity

Common equity is ownership that entitles the holder to residual cash flow and voting rights.

As you can see from the continuum each level of capital gave cash to the business (the productive asset) at the time of the investment and in return expects a return out of the future cash flow the productive asset produces to varying degrees with varying levels of "security" or "comfort" that they will receive their investment back. Conceptually you can think of this as a cash flow waterfall. As the productive asset produces cash flow that cash flow flows out to various investors in accordance with the various rates of return they are entitled to based on the type of risk they accepted when they contributed their units of exchange to the enterprise. As you work your way down the capital structure you increase your expected return, but decrease the certainty that you will receive the future return expected.

The Capital Structure and Financial Engineering

As you might also expect, clever financial engineers are quite talented at manipulating the capital structure of assets to make it appear a productive asset is performing better than it actually is or that return is more certain than it actually is.

The current gamesmanship in this year 2019, is the share-buyback. A number of years ago, board of directors looking to attract top talent to managerial and executive roles in business's came up with the idea of providing "stock options". The idea being if the executive worked for a certain period of time for the corporation their "stock options" would vest in that individual in accordance with certain time and performance metrics. The better the executive made the corporation perform the higher the company's value would be and therefore the higher the price the corporation should demand in the market for its stock. This would benefit all shareholders because they would have received the benefit of growth from good management by its executives and the executive would benefit because their pay would increase commensurate with their performance, while giving them an "ownership stake" in the company which should align their interests with the company's performance long-term. A "win-win" as business types like to say.

However, as with most good ideas, it did not take executive management long to figure out that even if their corporation's growth was struggling they could still make stock performance improve by leveraging the corporation with unhealthy levels of debt. Additionally, they could further juice their pay-packages by using the debt the company received to "buy-back" their own corporate equity. That is to say, the corporation would take a loan to be used for the purpose of purchasing its own equity. When a corporation purchases its own equity, that equity goes to the corporation's "treasury". That is to say, a corporation can't own itself, so that share of equity is just removed from the market.

As we discussed earlier all productive assets are evaluated based on their earnings. To determine how a business is performing per share, individuals look to "earnings per share", since EPS puts things in perspective based on how much an individual shareholder owns. Earnings per share is a ratio, the denominator of which is the total number of outstanding shares. Thus, if one cannot increase "earnings" through organic growth or debt growth, one can still give the appearance of increased performance by manipulating the denominator of the EPS ratio by decreasing the outstanding number of shares. Doing so, increases the stock price (which gives the appearance of productive growth – even if there is no productive growth) and allows these corporate executives to increase their pay packages.

The lower the interest rate on debt, the more it makes "sense" to do this, because you are in mathematical terms essentially capturing the cashflow spread we described back in Chapter 8. That is to say if you can take a loan out at 4% and use that money to buy an asset that produces 10%, you get the benefit of 6% of something you couldn't afford. In this case, what can't be afforded is the enterprise's own shares, but as long as those shares generate a return (or appear to generate a return) greater than the cost of the loan it makes financial "sense" to do so.

The danger of course is that this is a negative feed-back loop. Taking on debt and purchasing my own shares, increases my earnings per share, which gives the appearance of growth, which induces lenders to lend me more based on my increasing EPS growth and resulting increasing share price. This feed-back loop continues, until an earnings set back occurs (which will inevitably occur because there is no actual growth being prioritized with this additional leverage, but rather superficial non-sustainable, non-real growth), at which point lenders realize that the corporation is levered with more debt than it could sustain even in a positive growth environment and the debt begins to default. Almost all debt has a "cross-default" provision, that is to say, if any debt defaults other lenders have the ability to also default their loans as a safeguard for their debt investment and as such, things tend to spiral out of control quickly. As lenders tend to default all at the same time which further exacerbates the fact the corporation is having earnings growth issues.

Similarly, a significant amount of price inflation has occurred as a result of private equity, which largely follow leveraged buy-out models (most are in fact called "buy-out funds" for this reason). Buy-out funds work by the cash flow formula we described back in Chapter 8. Effectively, a productive asset is evaluated for its cash flow. It is then bought with debt at extremely favorable terms which is then securitized out through the securitization chain (and often packaged together into "structured products" that are sold as being safer than they actually are, usually to systemically important financial institutions, private credit funds and pension funds, so the originator offloads the risk of the loan and cares little for the ultimate loans performance). The private equity firm for its part enjoys the benefit of enhanced cash-on-cash return the more debt they are able to use to purchase an asset at the lowest interest rate they can negotiate. In a low risk-free rate environment, lenders are increasingly inclined to provide these loans because of the relative "safety" of the fund (depending on the monetary size of the fund, the number of investors, and the sophistication or institutional nature of such investors), the fact that the risk of the loan is securitized and offloaded in any case to debt investors who are supposed to "diversify" their risk (although are ironically typically composed of the same institutional customers who are invested in the private equity side of the business or similar situated private equity funds) and the general lack of being able to generate significant lending returns elsewhere.

If the productive asset fails to perform after the return on the productive asset is received the equity is no longer aligned with the debt, and the equity either resells the asset to someone else, or leaves the asset for dead under its debt burden (though all this time the manager making the decision has little "skin in the game" in any case, other than some reputational risk if their funds always leave a path of waste in their wake).

As noted earlier, the use of leverage in this manner makes returns look better in private equity (relative to other markets, typically public markets), so lenders increasingly desire to lend into what is perceived as a "better market" or "growing industry", although the growth is really debt fueled, which increases the purchase price of the underlying asset because the increase in credit makes equity believe that these assets have increased in value and now deserve higher purchase prices (the more cynical might conclude the managers just don't care since they have no skin in the game anyway). This self-fulfilling cycle continues quite happily and profitably until the risk-free rate changes such that either the rates of return on the underlying assets decrease until investment is unattractive to equity investors (since the spread between the equity return and the cost of the debt decreases), or corporations start to fail in mass under their debt burdens (or both). This in part is one of the reasons everyone is so finnicky about the Federal Reserve's desire to raise rates in this year 2019 (since movement of the risk-free rate will cause all assets to reprice in any event). To be clear, the decision makers, i.e. the private equity firms and asset managers (benefiting from bankruptcy remoteness) will be fine either way. They are not holding the bag. The lenders, institutional equity holders and the underlying assets are the ones most likely to suffer (of which the aging retiree who has paid into his/her pension his/her entire life is the most sympathetic).

Chapter 11: Risk and Correlative Return

As you can see from the continuum of risk, risk is correlated with return. As risk increases, expected return increases. This makes sense mathematically (and instinctively) because in order to induce an investor to buy an asset of greater risk than the risk-free rate such investor will need to be compensated with additional return accordingly.

Return can vary some in the same class of risk assets based on how well an individual investor values a company, analyzes cash flow, and pays a reasonable and appropriate purchase price, but generally speaking on a scale falls into a range of percentage return based on the type of risk sought. In the current low-inflation low-risk free rate environment, generally speaking the following percentage returns can be expected:

> US Government debt (risk-free rate and duration risk) will provide between 2% and 3% return depending on the duration (as duration extends price increases, although in this year 2019 treasuries have experienced yield curve inversion as previously mentioned).
>
> Investment grade debt will provide between 3-5% (most likely 4%) return. It should be noted that in this year 2019 a lot of debt rated investment grade (particularly debt in the BBB range) is not investment grade. It has been stripped of customary covenants and protections and security (some are in fact unsecured although they have through various structuring the appearance of senior secured debt on their face).

High yield debt will provide between 5-8% (most likely 7%) return. The high-yield market has increased greatly in-size due to the fact that 7%-8% return is considered a relatively standard return required by most investors, yet because the risk-free rate is so low (at around 2%) investors are increasingly inclined to take this risk (even though the risk probably outweighs the potential return at this point in the business cycle).

Mezzanine debt will yield between 7-12% (between 10-19% including equity incentives).

Preferred equity will yield 7-12% (between 10-15% including accrued returns and other kickers).

Common Equity will yield approximately >15% (although this depends greatly on the price at which the common equity is purchased, which is largely a factor of timing of when the purchase occurred in the lifecycle of the productive asset).

Generally speaking, the trade-off in this continuum is that if my productive asset fails, as a common equity holder I will receive nothing and as a secured creditor I will receive the salvage value of the productive asset (assuming there is any) to offset my loss. Conversely, as a common equity holder I am entitled to all residual profit and as a secured creditor, I am entitled to a contracted for interest rate. The center of the continuum between these extremes receives some mix of relative risk and return (i.e. as return becomes increasingly uncertain and recourse to recover principal minimizes the expected rate of return increases).

Chapter 12: Productive Growth v. Debt Growth and the Asymmetry of Risk

Now that an appropriate foundation has been laid, we can begin to discuss investment decision making. For purposes of our further discussion, we will primarily be concerned with investment in "common equity" unless otherwise stated.

As we have been alluding to throughout this book, there are two main price mismatches that are important to be aware of if one is going to invest successfully. The first is price v. value. As we have already discussed value is different from price. Investors who are successful, purchase assets at a price that doesn't reflect their value (that doesn't necessarily mean price is less than cash flow value, although it can, but rather means that people have incorrectly discounted price because of the myriad of factors associated with determining price, such that the price doesn't appropriately reflect the intrinsic value of the productive asset). As already discussed, price will typically be a multiple of future earnings. That is to say, price will typically contain within it a premium over the value of the earnings the productive asset produces. In public markets, this is called the price to earnings multiple (more accurately however it is the price to EPS) and represents a multiplying factor that is applied to earnings to arrive at price.

Because there are numerous factors that affect price (most of which are both subjective and mimetic) price will often fluctuate even if the underlying EPS growth occurs steadily. As an example of why this might occur, assume for instance people have a view that EPS will grow rapidly in the 1st quarter (by 25%), slow in the 2nd quarter (to 5%

growth), rally in the 3rd quarter (to 15% growth), and stay flat in the 4th quarter (at 15% growth) for a totally yearly growth of 60%. Now let's say rather than grow at those expected rates, EPS grows at 15% in each of the four quarters of the year. We can see that mathematically in the year earnings grew steadily at a good rate right in line with expectations in a linear fashion. However, it is highly unlikely price rose steadily and linearly over that period. Rather, price likely dropped in the 1st quarter to reflect that earnings grew only by 15% and not the 25% expected, jumped in the 2nd quarter where earnings grew much faster than the 5% expected, and then stayed largely the same for the rest of the year as the price accurately reflected the final two expected quarters earnings growth (i.e. the final two quarters of earnings growth were "priced-in" to the share price after the second quarter and price thereby stayed stagnant).

This is a simplification of what actually occurs, as in reality on a smaller scale there would be some debate (being visualized in the price) between whether or not earnings would be met in each quarter (based largely on rampant speculation on a variety of other factors as external as the weather and more analytic soft-data like customer growth over the period that people use to try and get an idea of whether earnings will come in as expected), so there would be fluctuation between each quarter as well as well as the price fluctuation on the earning report dates which surprise the market as being outside of expectations.

Sticking with our simpler example for the time being, one can see that even though earnings grew in a linear fashion. Price did not. Price fluctuated such that if you purchased shares of the stock in the 1st quarter after earnings were reported surprising the market negatively. You would have purchased at a much better price than if you purchased in the second quarter after the price recovered with the positive surprise, even though over the year period earnings were as steady as can be (linear in fact).

We will discuss using this mismatch between price and value to one's advantage in more detail later on, but for now, it should be clear that price tends to be more volatile than earnings, because price is derived from much more speculative factors than earnings (and any speculative components of calculating forward earnings contribute to additional volatility in price).

In our example above, I used a public stock equity, but it is important to note for clarity that the variation between price and value is true for any productive asset that can be bought or sold. The volatility in price will vary (in terms of both amplitude of volatility and the frequency of volatility) based on the availability of price information, the consistency of the modelling of cash flow, the general volatility of cash flow, the relative variability of supply and demand as well as other factors, but some degree of volatility in price is generally speaking true for all asset classes. A bond for instance will pay exactly the interest rate it says it will if you buy it at issuance, but during the time you hold it its market price will fluctuate based on the attractiveness of any new issuances and any variation in the risk free rate (or generally any change in the perceived certainty of the continued cash flow), among other factors. For now, however, we will continue to focus on equity because it is conceptually simpler to price.

Focusing in on earnings now, it is important to note that the nature by which earnings are derived are an important factor in determining the certainty that earnings are likely to continue in the future. Mainly are earnings a result of structural growth or a result of leveraged growth.

Earnings can grow as a result of compounding or put another way, because the productivity of an asset is growing. In a business this may take the form of an increasing consumer base. More customers results in more revenue (called "top line growth"), and if costs are controlled, more net cash flow which thereby increases earnings (called "bottom line growth"). Typically, bottom line growth translates into a higher price of the asset in the marketplace.

Much like the cells in the lab, this growth is organic productive sustainable growth, which will continue until the medium for growth runs out (i.e. the business runs out of new customers). In our hen example, our chicken farm grew because each reproductive cycle we kept some hens with which we could make more chickens. This provides sustainable productive growth until I run out of chicken farm, chicken food, enough workers to feed my chickens, customers to purchase my chickens or some disruptive technology comes that replaces the need for chickens (or can produce them or their byproducts faster and with a better quality than my hen farm). Generally speaking, if earnings are growing revenue should be growing commensurately in a healthy organization. (Although the converse may not be true, just because revenue grows, doesn't not necessarily mean earnings will grow because costs may have increased disproportionately, mismanagement, or profits may have been reinvested in the business for capital improvements (colloquially termed "capital expenditures")).

Earnings growth can also grow as a result of increasing the use of leverage to maximize returns. Debt growth can be productive, as previously discussed, because it lets you acquire productive assets you need, while deferring the purchase price, however when left unchecked it can also give a false sense of growth.

By way of example, using debt to buy-back shares will give the impression of earnings growth even though revenue (top line growth) will not have increased at all, all the while saddling the business with additional debt expense it will need to pay off in the future (and may not be able). Taking on additional debt for capital expenditures that exceed the demand for my product could also cause solvency issues. In my hen example, if I expect great demand for my chickens, I might take out a large loan secured by my hens to build an addition to my chicken farm. If thereafter the consumer need for chickens falls away, I may not be able to generate the cash flow to pay off my loan for those capital expenditures. At this point, the lenders might step in and take my current assets (mainly my chickens) away to settle the score for my not being able to pay back the loan.[32]

Debt while useful, can be dangerous because it risks today's assets for the benefit of future production which may or may not come. If that production does not come, I could be at risk of losing more than I had to gain. This risk

---

[32] Over expansion, i.e. expansion not in-line with consumer demand, historically, is among the most common reason for the failure of a business.

of loss is called the "asymmetry of risk" and is another pillar of investing. Generally speaking, the asymmetry of risk should always be in your favor. If I am going to take on a loan, I should be receiving the benefit of doubling my farm production for the sake of losing 20% of my chickens. No healthy business should ever be in danger of losing the entire farm for the sake of 10% more chicken production (and generally the entire farm should never be at risk).

Asymmetry of risk is another pillar that most people largely ignore, because other mimetic forces get in the way. When the farm is producing there is incentive to produce more and lenders will be willing to lend more because the farm is producing. They will encourage me to borrow, which in the short-term will benefit me with improved growth prospects. People will tell me I am brilliant and the best hen farmer in history, and I will not notice or care that I have taken on too much debt, because of course I, the brilliant hen farmer, will produce chickens in perpetuity for all the land; my chickens are better than everyone else's and demand for chickens will never cease.

The danger of course is when this asymmetry flips and one risks losing more than one is likely to gain or all that one has generally. Because this lending happens incrementally, however, it tends to creep up quietly before an individual even knows it is a problem. Inevitably growth stalls in all productive things (even if only for a time) and that can be a problem if I've bet the farm that growth won't ever stop during the great chicken mania of 2019[33].

---

[33] There is no great chicken mania occurring in this year of 2019 to my knowledge, this is merely an example. Although there has been a fair bit of mania in the cryptocurrency, biotechnology and technology

It is also notable that taking on a lot of debt in an asset's capital structure makes it vulnerable to fluctuations in the debt markets (mainly fluctuations in interest rates), which could take a sustainable debt service ratio and make it unsustainable (even though as a chicken farmer I likely haven't spent any portion of my education learning about the risk free rate and its effects).

Conversely, if one keeps the asymmetry of risk in mind, leverage is great. It boosts purchasing power in the present, which boosts future productivity and although temporary "death" events or reductions in growth are experienced, on the whole, over time the enterprise continues to grow, never losing more than it stands to gain. Despite various cycles, the asset grows with time, compounding until it is quite successful.

As you might expect, knowing whether growth is mostly productive or mostly debt is helpful to know because it allows you to see if growth is healthy and sustainable. To be sure having a debt load is not intrinsically bad, but if the asymmetry flips you can be fairly confident that you will get defaults and a reversion to the mean when the market is considered as a whole. This is true for any productive asset, but is perhaps most interesting when considered on a total economic scale (since people take great pleasure in predicting economic crisis and conditions generally). Therefore, as a visual aide I have attached a series of charts below which provide information on the economy generally over a long-term time horizon. I will provide a brief explanation of my interpretation of each below.

---

sectors, which exhibit similar egotism to the chicken mania I describe here facetiously.

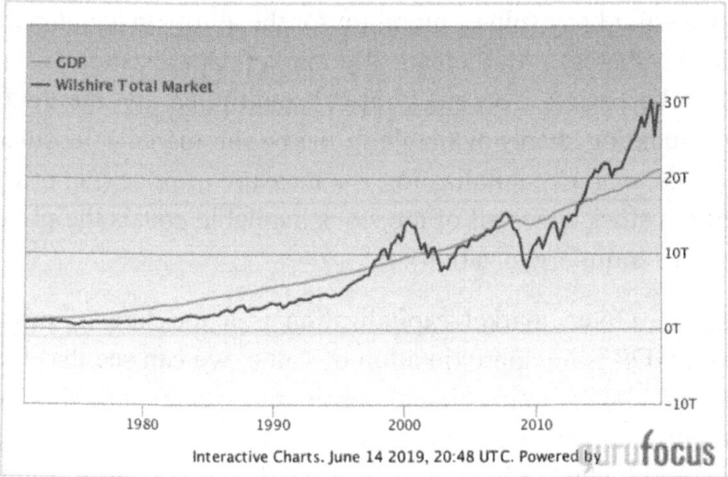

34

The chart above illustrates the global domestic product (GDP) of the United States of America and the "Wilshire Total Market" index. GDP is the total value of goods produced and services provided in an economy. It is a measure of a total economy's domestic production and therefore serves as a fair approximation of the "value" of an economy. That is to say, GDP measures the production of the productive asset that is the economy (in this case the US economy). The Wilshire Total Market index is designed to measure the market value of all US stocks traded in the US. That is to say, the Wilshire Total Market index is intended to track the "market capitalization" of all US stocks actively traded on public markets in the US. "Market Capitalization" is a measure of a public stock's total "price" (often stated erroneously as a public stock

[34] https://www.gurufocus.com/stock-market-valuations.php

corporation's total "value", but as we know value and price are not the same). If you were going to purchase an entire public stock corporation, its market capitalization is what you would pay (plus a premium for the ability to acquire all of the shares). Mathematically market capitalization is the "market price" (or stock price) multiplied by the total outstanding shares available in the public market. In other words, market capitalization is a measure of price (i.e. price of the stock times all of the stock available equals the price of the entire organization).

Given market capitalization is a measure of price and GDP is an approximation of value, we can see that the chart above (on national economic scale) graphically represents whether the economy is priced higher or lower than its value. Based on the chart above, we can see that between the 1980s and most of the 1990s, the price of public stocks was lower than the relative value being produced by the economy (although inflation was running rampant during most of the 80s which was eroding value as we will discuss briefly below). In the late 1990s early 2000s, the price of public stocks exceeded the relative value being produced by the economy (as you probably remember the increase in the price of stocks was fueled largely by a bubble in technology stocks, which while new, innovative and explosive creators of new value, were also largely over-hyped). After the technology bubble collapse (in the early 2000s), the price of public stocks once again fell below the relative value being produced by the national economy. This mismatch to price and value continued until around 2006-2007, when price once again exceeded relative value of GDP (this time largely due to the creation of the securitization chain and various innovative financial products, which while they created value, were much riskier than they were marketed as and thereby purchased by uninformed people whose investment needs required safety rather than return). After the financial crisis, the market price of public stocks once again sunk below the relative productive value of the US economy. This continued until around 2014-2015 at which point the market price of public stocks began exceeding the relative productive value of the US economy and has continued to widen until the present year (2019 at the time of this writing).

As can be seen from the discussion above, despite the simplicity of the chart, because of our understanding of the difference between "price" and "value" it is fairly easy to see whether market prices are relatively "expensive" or "cheap" on the whole relative to the productive value of the market, by taking a view of 1) whether the price is higher or lower than the relative value of the market and 2) the magnitude by which the price is higher or lower than the relative value of the market (i.e. the spread or distance between the two charted lines) or said another way, how expensive or cheap the market price is relative to the underlying productive value. This is a powerful tool and while it doesn't have any "predictive" ability (that is to say it won't tell you whether or not a boom or recession is imminent) knowing whether things generally are over-priced relative to value is an extremely powerful tool for an investor to have at the outset. Additionally, because the Federal Reserve Bank of St. Louis provides this information and keeps it updated, it is quite simple at any time to get a clear picture of the relative price to value of the US public equity markets.[35]

[35] To be clear, a comparison of price to value of an asset can be

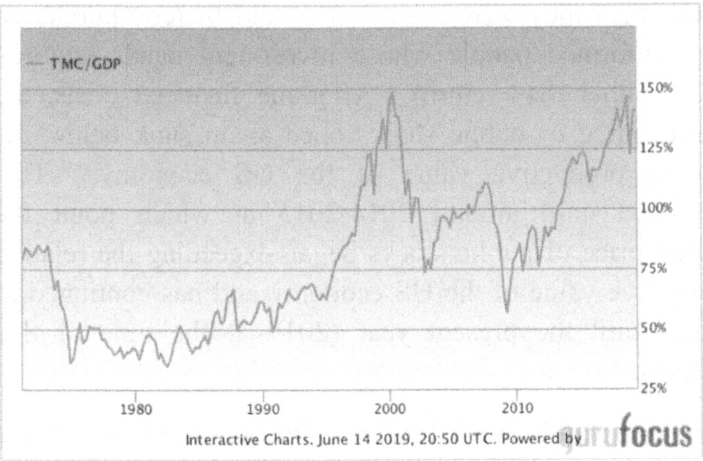

[36]

The chart above is the same chart of the Wilshire Total Market Index and GDP as we discussed above, except it is expressed as a ratio. That is to say, rather than chart the Wilshire Total Market Index and GDP on the same chart, the Wilshire Total Market Index was divided

---

conducted in a number of ways beyond the analysis discussed above. As an example, one could generate a similar metric of relative "expensiveness" or "cheapness" of the U.S. public equity markets by taking the price of a U.S. index (such as the S&P index) and dividing such price by the earnings of all of the components of the index averaged together and averaged over a period of years. A common metric of this kind is the Shiller CAPE ratio (which adjusts for inflation and averages earnings over a trailing 10-year period to account for average earnings over a full business cycle) for which, among other things, Robert Shiller won a Nobel Prize. Similarly, for individual assets, it was a hallmark of Benjamin Graham's investment strategy to divide the price of any given asset by its average earnings over a set time interval to get a relative sense of the "expensiveness" or "cheapness" of that security (averaging earnings overtime having the effect of removing any volatility in earnings or corporate manipulation of earnings in the short-term which might otherwise distort a P/E multiple).

[36] https://www.gurufocus.com/stock-market-valuations.php

by GDP to create a ratio of price to value. On a percentage basis, expression as a ratio is useful, because it readily shows the difference or spread between price and value. Expression as a percentage also has the effect of normalizing the real growth numbers to a set scale. From the chart above, it is easy to see that when Total Market Capitalization to GDP ratio is greater than 100% (i.e. the price of public stocks is double the productive value of the U.S. economy) the market tends to be "expensive" or "over-priced".

Value and Growth – Productive and Debt

Taking a step back for a minute, it is also important to note that overtime the US economy tends to grow in value. Despite the fluctuations in price in the market (that made the market periodically over- or under-priced), the value of the U.S. economy grew because global domestic product grew. As a real world example, if you purchased shares in the U.S. economy as a whole, in the 1980s, the price at which you could sell those shares today far exceeds the cost to you in 1980, despite the fact you would have lived through two "stock market bubbles", because productive value over that time increased. In the U.S. value tends to increase with time because the U.S. has stable currency, a robust legal framework in which people can be generally comfortable their assets are safe from others who would harm or steal their assets (which encourages investment and risk taking), the population (and therefore available workforce) tends to grow over time (due to increasing birth rates relative to death rates[37] and a

---

[37] In recent times, this ratio of birth rate to death rate has steadily declined causing a fair bit of concern among economists and long-term investors.

generally permissive policy toward immigration), the population is largely educated/possesses productive skills[38] and the U.S. economic system prioritizes innovation (among a few other factors as well). As a result, throughout history it has been a safe bet that the U.S. domestic economy's productive value will grow with time. To be clear, this does not have to be the case (and over short periods of time this is in fact not the case), however historically the U.S. social framework is designed for sustainable growth over a long period of time.

To be clear, despite the fact that overtime the U.S. economy tends to grow in productive value consistently, over a shorter time horizon the U.S. economy's productive value does fluctuate. That is to say growth of the U.S. economy (like all productive assets) has a life-cycle which includes growth and "death" phases. This is referred to colloquially as the "business-cycle" and tends to follow a general pattern of 10 years (roughly 7-10 years of growth to 1-3 years of decay).

To measure whether or not the U.S. economy is growing ("expanding") or dying ("contracting"), one looks to the "rate of change" in the U.S. economy's growth year to year (the data is in practice gathered quarterly and compiled annually). As you might remember from calculus, the "rate of change" is a measure of "velocity" that is to say the speed at which one is moving and is a derivative of "distance", i.e. how far something has moved.

---

[38] In recent times, the rate at which technology is advancing relative to the number of workers with skills necessary to work in technologically advanced industries (a so-called "skills gap") is another factor which has caused a fair bit of concern among economists and long-term investors.

In real terms, the chart above was illustrative of "nominal GDP" that is to say, the numerical value of the GDP of the U.S. We could see visually that the line charting GDP was rising (i.e. it had a positive slope) so we could see intuitively that it was "growing" with time. The "rate of change" is the measure of that slope of the line. That is to say, from year to year, what is the rate of growth or how fast is the numerical value of GDP growing or increasing.

If the rate of GDP growth is a positive number (greater than zero), nominal GDP is growing (and the slope of the line is positive and therefore tilted up). If the rate of GDP growth is a negative number (less than zero), nominal GDP is shrinking (and the slope of the line is negative and therefore tilted down). If the rate of GDP growth is zero, nominal GDP stayed the same from the year before (to be clear there was still production, it was just production at the same amount as the year before and therefore the line was flat with a slope of zero). When GDP growth is positive or zero, the U.S. economy is considered to be in an expansion phase (or recovery phase if the growth follows a recession). When GDP growth is negative, the U.S. economy is considered to be in a "recession".[39]

[39] Technically speaking, a "recession" is defined as two consecutive quarters of declining economic growth as determined by the National Bureau of Economic Research (and GDP growth does not necessarily need to be negative for the Nation Bureau of Economic Research to make this determination).

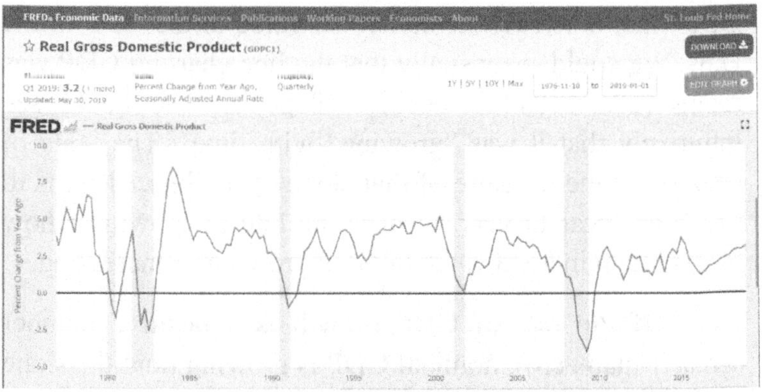

[40]

The chart above, from the Federal Reserve Bank of St. Louis, shows the growth rate of GDP since the 1980s. It is in fact, a chart of the slope of the GDP charted in the first graph we viewed in this chapter (it is a derivative of the first chart in calculus terms). As you can see, the growth rate has fluctuated somewhere between approximately -3.0% and 8% during that time period. For the most part, the U.S. economy during this time period enjoyed growth for 10 years for every 3 years of negative growth. Additionally, the growth experienced during those 10 year increments tended to far exceed the negative growth or lack of growth experienced during the 3 year increments. Thus, overtime despite the temporary 3-year blips, on the whole the U.S. GDP (i.e. the value of the U.S. economy) grew during the period beginning in 1980. Looking back at the first chart of nominal GDP, this is quite apparent, as nominal GDP is charted with an upward sloping line that every 3 years has a downward "blip", which reverses and continues upward over time (ending at a much higher level than it started at in the 1980s).

[40] https://fred.stlouisfed.org/graph/?g=eUmi

Mathematically, this is the case because 1) the magnitude of the negative rate of changes tends to be less than the magnitude of the positive rate of changes and 2) the time period of the negative rate of changes tends to be less than the time period of the positive rate of changes. Said another way, the U.S. tends to experience more positive GDP growth over a longer period of time than negative GDP growth, which tends to occur over shorter periods. The U.S. tends to grow in value more than it loses it and tends to grow in value for longer than it loses it.

To be clear, the GDP number that is often reported in financial news is GDP growth and not nominal GDP. GDP growth is interesting to financial minded individuals because changes in the rate of change from time period to time period can be indicative of future expansions or recessions. Mathematically, measurement of the rate of change in the rate of change is a derivative of the rate of change and second derivative of nominal GDP. Said in physics terms, GDP measures distance, the rate of change measures velocity, and the rate of change of the rate of change (which is the second derivative of GDP), measures "acceleration". Acceleration is interesting because before velocity changes from positive to negative, its acceleration will tend to change. That is to say, it is fairly rare to have positive GDP growth of 5% and then suddenly negative GDP of -2.5%. What is more common is for there to be a slowing period in which GDP growth goes from 5% to 3% to 1% to 0 to -2.5%. If you recognize that the rate of change in GDP is slowing when it is still at 3%, you can act more readily to protect yourself against recessions and periods of contraction.

Using a car as an example (which exhibits all the same laws of physics as growth and decay). If you are traveling 60 mph and someone slams on the brakes. You don't go from 60mph to zero mph immediately. If someone slams the breaks you may go from 60mph to 40mph to 20mph to 0mph over a very short period of time, but you will be aware that you are slowing down before you stop moving entirely (unless you crash). Similarly, a typical driver will tend not to slam the brakes from 60mph to 0mph but will rather most often coast to a halt. Thus, if you are aware of changes in acceleration, you can begin to prepare yourself for stopping. (It should also be mentioned, however, that just like a car, the driver could press the gas again after slowing down only to 40mph and reaccelerate up to 60mph, so you cannot be 100% sure you are stopping every time someone hits the break pedal. However, being aware of acceleration is still helpful generally, provided you don't freak out about it every time someone hits the brake.)

In addition to being aware of acceleration, it is also helpful to know why GDP is growing. That is to say is growth in GDP based on "sustainable" or "organic" growth or is it a result of increasing amounts of debt.

GDP growth based on sustainable or "organic" growth is subject to a growth cycle (as discussed earlier in this book), however it is more sustainable and less likely to cause issues until costs of production become unsustainable, the market becomes saturated (i.e. the economy runs out of consumers) or demand for U.S. products/services decreases. Generally speaking, on a national scale it takes a great deal of time for organic growth to end and when it does end, it generally does not decay to less of a value position than with which the cycle began. That is to say, even though the economy might suffer some loss or decay, the value of the productive asset that is the U.S. economy remains at a level of production that matches the relative demand and costs to produce the supply. This is known as an "equilibrium" and is not terribly problematic for any productive asset. The one exception to this is a new "disruptive" technology that completely replaces the demand for a particular productive asset, however on a national scale, "disruptive" innovation is typically a net positive (although it sometimes causes a short-term negative affect) because the new productive asset tends to be superior to the prior productive asset and tends to increase overall value over time (by either reducing cost, increasing demand, or increasing capacity).[41]

GDP growth based on debt is subject to a "debt cycle" (which loosely tracks and typically overlays the "growth cycle") and tends to be less sustainable and more disruptive during "decay" periods. The primary reason for this is the nature of debt discussed earlier and revisit below for the sake of clarity.

---

[41] As an example, it seems likely that artificial intelligence and machine learning will disrupt many industries over the next few years. In so doing, it is likely to displace many workers, which typically would be considered a negative for U.S. economic production as many workers will likely become unproductive. However, because artificial intelligence and machine learning will likely make businesses highly efficient (reducing costs while increasing production) it is probable that artificial intelligence and machine learning will likely increase U.S. economic production and GDP on the whole (although it will also likely cause widespread income inequality as profits are concentrated in economic owners of enterprises at the expense of displaced workers).

For equity, debt increases purchasing power today in return for paying a cost (if done correctly out of earnings) in the future. As already noted, future earnings are inherently speculative and subject to a growth cycle, so there is a scenario (depending on the timing of when debt is taken on in the growth cycle and the amount of debt taken on) in which future earnings will be insufficient to pay off the borrowed money used today (or at least make it less likely lenders will be willing to allow borrowing in the future because earnings didn't perform as well and weren't as "safe" as expected).

In a default scenario (where the equity is unable to pay back the lenders), the lenders will foreclose on collateral (assuming they are secured lenders) and the equity will lose some (potentially all) of their productive assets to repay their debt, which makes them less able to generate future returns since their supply of productive assets has been decreased (perhaps completely foreclosed upon). In a non-defaulting scenario, a lack of sufficiently robust earnings could make lenders less willing to lend to the same enterprise in the future (which will likely have the effect of reducing future growth, because the enterprise will no longer have the benefit of leverage in growing). If management is in the practice of continually having an amount of leverage on the productive asset, diminished or declining earnings could make lenders less willing to maintain these ordinary debt levels (in colloquially speak, less willing to refinance the debt or "roll over" the debt). During times of growth, debt helps to grow faster, but in times of decline, it hastens the decline and perhaps causes ultimate demise, if the lenders have the ability and desire to take all of the productive assets. Returning to our car example, debt is analogous to a turbo charger with nitrous oxide in it. It will get you wherever you are going faster than you could with only your engine, but if allowed to overheat, it will also blow up the whole car (or at minimum cause damage to the engine). In most cases, debt makes a good situation better and a bad situation worse.

Because of our human nature, a productive asset is more likely to be given debt when it is at the end of its growth cycle because that is when productivity/earnings will look best and when there will have been a "track record" of success. This is also the worst time to take on debt or lend into an asset. Additionally, because no one wants to fail (and most are generally afraid of any kind of death or decay) once the growth starts to fade, management will try to maintain as much growth as possible, because they will feel pressure to service existing debt (and not become insolvent), which will become harder depending on how much earnings decline. In this scenario, management (typically poor managers) often try to take on more debt to service their old debt or to try and fuel additional growth (since stoking sustainable growth is harder than getting a new loan that covers up the deficiency in the immediate term). At this point, the growth rate of debt begins to exceed the growth rate of sustainable growth, or at minimum begins to take up an increasing portion of growth.

Referring back to our conversation of economic expansions and recessions, on a national scale, if debt growth is increasing its proportion of GDP growth, you can be fairly certain that the expansion period is nearing an end (or at least on dangerous footing). At its worst, debt growth will exceed GDP growth such that all or most of GDP growth is a result of debt growth (in such a situation without the additional debt growth GDP growth would actually be negative or said another way the economy would be in a recession absent the additional debt). This is a sure sign, that an expansion is beginning to collapse on itself, and will likely result in a more dramatic collapse because lenders will exacerbate declining revenue when they seek additional recourse on the non-performing assets (facilitating a more dramatic collapse than the "equilibrium" that would be reached if only sustainable growth was involved). It effectively, signifies a situation in which productive assets are running out of sustainable growth and the decision makers are covering up the problem by borrowing more (not unlike taking out new credit cards to pay off old credit cards because you have lost your job and have no income). It is a short-term fix to a long-term problem; one that makes the long-term problem worse.[42]

---

[42] Theoretically, the long-term solutions to such a problem would be to (1) generate organic sustainable growth such that an increase in earnings growth is sufficient to cover future debt service, (2) pay down outstanding debt or (3) refinance to make debt more manageable (either in duration by extending the term or by lowering the interest rate/cost of such debt). However, on both a business and global/national scale, it tends to be fairly difficult to sufficiently increase earnings sustainably to cover debt service when already overleveraged. On both a business and global/national scale paying down debt tends to have at least a short-term negative impact on growth, since debt is presumably paid down out of either current or retained earnings. Refinancing debt to make debt more manageable is potentially possible on a business level (assuming the business is otherwise fairly healthy and lenders are willing to participate in refinance existing debt), but tends to not be a feasible option on a global/national scale (that is to say, on a global/national scale it tends to take the form of increasing monetary supply through either additional debt issuance or some form of money printing, which tends to have an often harmful inflationary effect as discussed earlier).

As previously mentioned, the "business cycle" tends to last for approximately 10 years, which is likely related to the fact that the average growth-phase for the average business is approximately 10 years. Interestingly, the maturity of the average corporate loan is somewhere between 7-15 years. Thus, growth tends to top out, right where lenders are looking to de-risk which has the effect of exacerbating issues right at the end of most businesses' growth phases.

To evidence our discussion, I have attached the Corporate Debt to GDP ratio from the 1950s to the present, where "corporate debt" is the aggregate non-financial corporate debt. Once again, this is a ratio produced by dividing "corporate debt" by GDP. That is to say, it is a measure of the amount of corporate debt that makes up a part of GDP.[43]

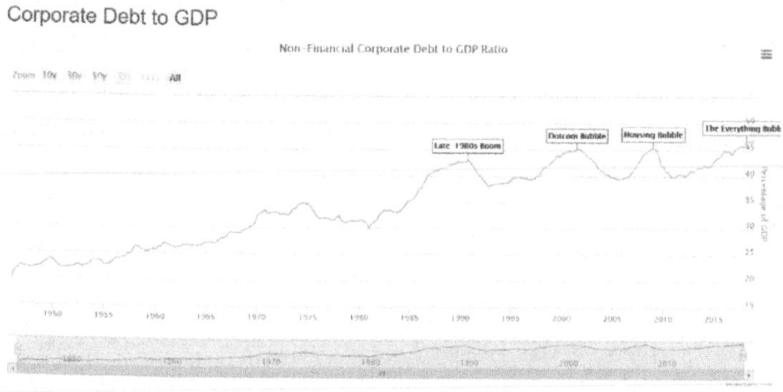

44

[43] It is mathematically feasible to make this comparison since debt generally can be considered a "productive asset". That is to say, lending money creates an accounting "asset" and the borrowed money is used productively, thus contributing to growth, if not real growth, growth at minimum in the monetary supply, because the borrowed money is counted twice, once as money used to buy something as value and once as an "asset" in the lender's loan book.

Focusing in on the 1990s to the present, it is readily evident that debt makes up the largest portion of GDP, at the very end of each business cycle and tends to precede a recession (it in effect assists in causing a recession, by exacerbating declining growth). It is also notable that, in addition to the short-term 10 year debt cycles visible on the chart, debt as a proportion of GDP has steadily grown with time over the last 70 years.

As will become more evident later in this book, all markets (including the debt markets) are fractals. That is to say, markets are made up of multiple time periods of recurring cycles (small cycles which grow into larger cycles). In addition to the short-term 10 year business cycle and 10 year short-term debt cycle, there also tends to be a roughly 40 - 100 year long-term economic cycle and a long-term debt cycle spanning roughly the same time period. This is largely due to the fact inflation cycles (and thereby monetary supply/interest rate cycles which tend to prioritize lending/saving to different degrees) tend to take somewhere between 40-100 years and tend to prioritize different degrees of risk-taking.

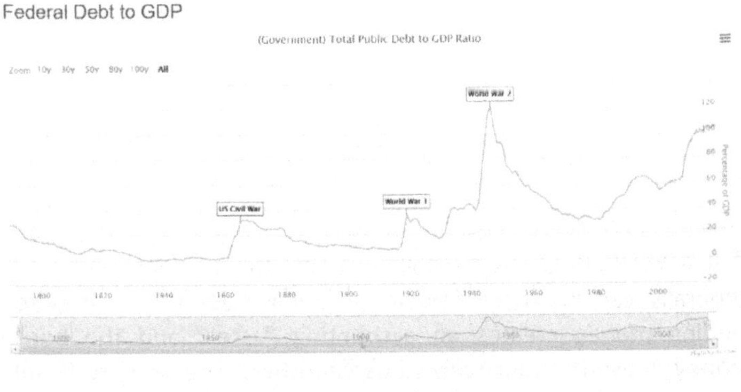

45

---

[44] https://www.longtermtrends.net/us-debt-to-gdp-ratios/

As can be seen from the Federal Debt to GDP ratio, long-term social views on public and private debt cycle with time and tend to correlate with conflicts between economies and governments on a global scale (at their most dramatic resulting in war, socio-political and currency crises).[46]

Price Fluctuations and the Return of the Risk-Free Rate

As we have seen above, despite the fact the U.S. economy, because of its general political, legal and social structure, tends to enjoy productive growth over time, value does fluctuate in accordance with the growth-cycle of the productive assets which aggregate to form the overall economy's business cycle. As we have also discussed, price, while underpinned by value, tends to fluctuate more dramatically than value because price is inherently speculative. That is to say, price is based on speculative views on future earnings, comparisons to other similar assets, supply and demand, and a variety of other external factors that have nothing to do with the inherent productive value of an asset, not the least of which are mimetic forces (which at their base aren't even rational, but rather based on the irrationality of human desire). Additionally, because

---

[45] https://www.longtermtrends.net/us-debt-to-gdp-ratios/

[46] I will not discuss the nature of these cycles or their global-macroeconomic impact in any great detail in this book, but would recommend Ray Dalio's "Understanding Major Debt Crises." for further reading, if this is of particular interest to the reader. To be clear, I have no association with Ray Dalio other than to say I have read this particular book of his and think it is a fantastic explanation of debt cycles. I would generally recommend it for anyone who desires to understand how debt cycles work and affect economies and global politics.

opposed to "wall street") will become interested in the asset because it has either hit the mainstream news and main-street investors are aware of it or because they have seen other people gain profit from it and desire to share in that profit (i.e. the mimetic process begins to set in). (At such point, investors who were part of the early growth phase of the asset, tend to sell their interests into the rising demand created by less sophisticated investors.)

It is at this point, that management typically takes on more debt to attempt to juice the rate of return to warrant the price the productive asset now fetches as a result of the mimetic process. It is also at this point, that expected future earnings will become increasingly disconnected from underlying value. Future growth will be expected based solely on past growth (which is no guarantee of future return) and the prospect of decay will be generally expelled as erroneous thinking. (During this time period, analysts, who would otherwise know better, often continue to take highly optimistic views on earnings, because they are incentivized to do so on the basis that if they do not give good projections and projections turn out better than expected their cynicism will get them fired whereas if they take an optimistic view and are wrong they will retain their job as long as everyone else is optimistic. As a result, analyst opinions tend to lag actual price movement, since it is safer to do so from a retention of employment perspective).[47] Eventually, the productive

[47] You might recognize this as herding behavior typical of humans (and most animals for that matter) which is based on the belief that it is safer in the pack than outside of the pack. In the context of financial markets, this pack mentality results in a historically abysmal record for predictive forecasting among analysts and economists. In most cases statistically speaking, you would be better served to flip a coin and use

asset, hits a decaying phase and the increased debt load exacerbates this problem which causes a decline in price (as people scramble to the exit to prevent losing money associated with purchasing an asset at too high a price). As you might expect, crowded selling creates stampede-like behavior which further exacerbates the sell off.

The end result of the mimetic process I have described above, is that toward the end of a productive asset's growth phase, people will be overly optimistic and tend to exaggerate the future earnings growth prospects of a productive asset. As a result, if one purchases at such a time period, one may pay more in price than one will be able to receive in earnings value over a reasonable time period. That is to say, it is quite possible for someone to pay a premium equivalent to 20 years future revenue growth as a purchase price, have the productive asset enter a decay phase where the price declines dramatically and 10 years later remain in a loss position because another 10 years is required to regain the purchase price. Additionally, this may occur even if the asset is never really "non-productive", that is to say that much like our earnings example earlier on in this chapter, speculation of 20 years earnings, could (and will likely correct) to 10 years earnings, if earnings growth doesn't rise as quickly as expected in the short term (even if it still does in fact rise and the productive asset never experiences a decline in earnings "growth").

The technology bubble of the 2000s is a good example of the situation described in the paragraph above. There was a major price bubble in the 2000s that burst (a

---

the coin's result as a predictive forecast than to listen to the opinion of an economist or analyst.

result of overvalued technology firms that had no earnings of any kind and in some cases no revenue), yet this bubble burst without GDP ever becoming negative (i.e. without the U.S. economy ever failing to grow). The mere adjustment in the expectation of future earnings at a slower growth rate than was anticipated was sufficient to cause the price bubble to burst. To be clear, even though price collapsed dramatically and eroded value, GDP growth never actually went negative. The deacceleration of GDP growth was enough on its own to cause the price bubble to deflate, because the decreased rate of growth was out of line with expectations of future earnings.

The other result of the mimetic process is that the most uninformed will tend to buy latest in the cycle and are at the most risk of loss. In fact, some investors actually use public opinion as a barometer of relative expense. That is to say, some investors become concerned that a market is over-valued, when people who have no understanding or interest in the market suddenly become interested in investing. This also tends to occur when the market reaches all-time highs, because such an event is deemed newsworthy by more mainstream outlets that non-financial people tend to watch. At this point the mimetic process kicks in and people who have no real understanding of financial markets begin believing they will receive a reward because other people have received one in the past, which has the result of driving up demand and as a result a price that is not warranted.

Additionally, because of the influence of "venture capital" in recent times some investors discount earnings as a measure of value entirely, instead opting to focus on customer growth or other non-cash flow metrics as a

investor purchases at a set interval (monthly or yearly). The end result of this strategy tends to be that by investing in a set interval, one purchases at both times of over-and under-pricing which has the effect of smoothing (or averaging) one's cost-basis in assets over time such that one is still able to effectively acquire the increase in underlying value experienced by underlying GDP growth.

Through most of the preceding chapter, we have been evaluating relative "expensiveness" by analyzing the difference between price and underlying "value", using market capitalization and nominal GDP as a proxy. However, it is important to mention that while market capitalization to GDP is a helpful metric, it does not tell the entire story because it doesn't account for the "risk-free rate". As we've already discussed all assets are valued relative to the risk-free rate. That is to say, the attractiveness of the return of any investment will depend upon the relative return one could generate without taking any risk.

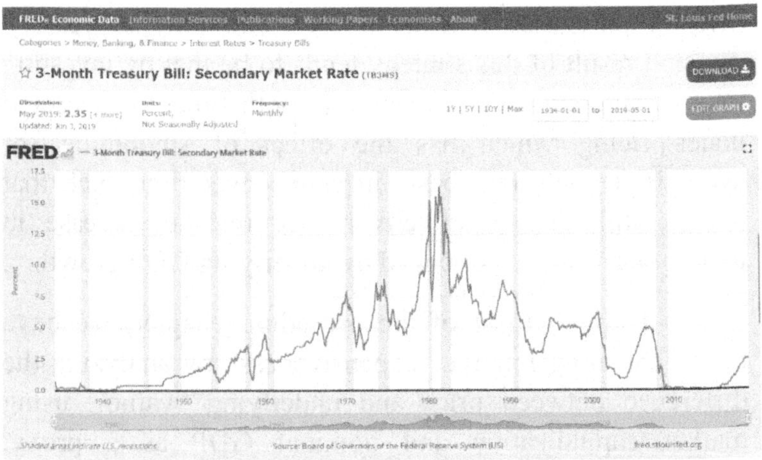

51

As can be seen from the chart above, the risk-free rate is subject to mimetic cycles (as the risk-free rate is moved by market forces like inflation and is manipulated by the Federal Reserve Board to promote or restrain economic activity to smooth boom-bust cycles). As mentioned earlier, movement in the risk-free rate has a powerful effect on lending rates (which itself contributes to both short-term and long-term debt cycles) by setting the floor rate on top of which all lending is based (most loans are given at the risk free rate plus a risk premium for the relative risk over the risk free rate).

Putting the role of the risk-free rate in the debt cycle (which as we have learned overlays and exacerbates the growth cycle of productive assets) aside for now, movement of the risk-free rate also has the effect of determining the relative worth of more risky assets. That is to say, if the risk-free rate is higher than one could expect

[51] https://fred.stlouisfed.org/series/TB3MS

to receive from a riskier asset the intelligent investor will choose the risk-free rate instead.

As an example, if the risk-free rate exceeds the return one would expect from equity returns, equity returns will become unattractive and less people will be willing to take the risk of equity (since they can get a commensurate return risk-free). This will give the appearance of underpricing on the market capitalization to GDP chart, since the lack of demand for equities will be reflected in lower prices relative to the value of GDP production, even though in reality the relative return of the equity markets is inferior to the return that can be generated risk-free. To be clear, this is not to say that the equity markets were not undervalued during periods of a high-risk free rate (because they are). It is that the reason for underpricing the equity is perfectly rational. That is to say, it is a better risk-to-return to take the risk-free rate during these periods. Additionally, a high-risk free rate tends to correlate with high inflation (that is to say the Federal Reserve typically raises rates to compensate lenders for higher inflation which would otherwise discourage lending, as discussed earlier) and as a result during periods of elevated risk-free rates, there tends to be a great deal of inflation which erodes the value of investments (like equities) which are denominated in that inflated currency.

As an example, in the 1980s it is easy to see that in nominal terms, the market price of equities was below the value of U.S. economic production. However, looking at our chart of the 3-month T-Bill we also see that during this period the risk-free rate was almost 15% (which is in-line with typical equity returns). As a result, even though the market price was relatively “cheap” by production standards, it was not "cheap" by return standards, since it was unlikely to perform better than the risk-free rate (despite having to accept much greater risk of loss in equities). As a result, in the 1980s the market capitalization of stocks could not really be considered "cheap". This changed when the risk-free rate began to decrease in the 1990s at which point, equity returns once again became attractive (and were still undervalued by price to value standards as seen in the chart of market capitalization to GDP at the beginning of this chapter).

The converse is also true. That is to say, during periods where the market otherwise appears overvalued by market capitalization to GDP standards, an extremely low risk-free rate could make accepting such equity risk more palatable and make otherwise "overvalued" market prices comparatively "fairly priced". This situation, however, is more dangerous than the prior inverse example discussed, because it prioritizes taking the risk of total loss as a result of the fact there is simply nowhere else to generate an adequate return more safely (which is a more hazardous risk-taking paradigm than taking no risk and receiving adequate return at the risk of missing out on a bit of additional return). Such an environment tends to lead individuals to ignore the asymmetry or risk or said another way to take risks where the potential gain is outweighed by the potential for loss.

Looking at 2010 through the present 2019 in the first chart in this chapter, it seems clear that by market capitalization to GDP standards, the market price of U.S. equities is over-priced. However, looking at the risk-free rate chart above, we see that the risk-free rate is at or near zero (and has been there for almost a 10-year period). As such, despite the fact the market appears over-priced, it might be considered "fairly valued" in comparative terms, because the alternative to taking equity risk is to receive almost nothing "risk-free". As you might expect this also encourages taking on debt by most borrowers (because borrowing costs are extremely low) and should in theory result in inflation (since extending credit is monetarily expansive, i.e. increases the relative money supply), which should cause the federal reserve to raise the risk free rate (to compensate lenders for eroding value and to encourage lending), which should cause a repricing of the equity markets as demand decreases as the risk-free rate becomes more attractive. In short, all return is subject to comparison to the risk-free rate and as such any movement in the risk-free rate necessarily reprices all other assets relative to these movements in the risk-free rate (that is to say, they become either more or less attractive, demand forces change and price relative to underlying value is affected).

By way of brief recap since we have covered a lot of ground, all productive assets are measured based on their ability to produce return, referred to as "earnings". All of the production of all of the productive assets in the U.S. economy is referred to as GDP which is therefore a measurement of the value of the U.S. economy. GDP growth is a measurement of the rate of change in GDP, that is to say whether the value of the U.S. economy is increasing or decreasing. It is important to know whether GDP is growing because of sustainable or organic growth or because of an expansion in debt, because knowing the difference can indicate whether growth is sustainable and likely to continue. Changes in the rate of change in GDP growth can also indicate whether or not GDP growth is likely to continue. Market prices are subject to speculative forecasts of future growth as well as mimetic forces and as such can either under-estimate or over-estimate the value of the U.S. economy. Market prices are inherently affected by the relative return they generate relative to the risk-free rate. Knowing whether market prices under-value or over-value the production of the U.S. economy and/or can reasonably be expected to produce returns in excess of the risk-free rate can increase the rate of return received by investors by permitting them to lower the purchase price of their investments, which increases the rate of return one can expect to receive by lowering the cost by which one acquires a right to future income. Generally speaking, all investors should be keeping an eye on market capitalization to GDP (whether in nominal terms or a ratio), the debt to GDP ratio, the risk-free rate, and the rate of change in GDP.

Before we move on to the next chapter, it is worth noting that visually we can see from the first chart in this chapter, that over-time price tends to revert to real underlying value. As we already discussed, this is a result of productive assets experiencing periods of "decay" at which times, an equilibrium of price will be reached which is more in-line with the productive asset's underlying value. The further price strays from value initially during its growth phase (as a result of mimetic forces), the more dramatic this reversion can be (the exception of course is if the increase in price is warranted by robust future value, which causes the value line to catch up to price, however because humans are mimetic creatures and price is more speculative, price tends to revert more quickly and more often than value catches up to price targets). This is a concept known as "reversion".

Many investors/traders use a "moving average", an average of price over a set time frame that continually adjusts as new data points become available (i.e. as time goes on) to approximate the true "value" of price. As we know, this is not a true measurement of value, but as an approximation tends to serve as a fair base for where the price of a productive asset should be on average relative to where it might be positioned on any given day. That is to say, it has a smoothing affect and tends to show when price is higher than its "average price" or lower than its "average price", which can be helpful to know. Overtime, price will tend to revert toward this average (or the average will catch-up to price) after periods of speculation away from its average. Typically investors and traders will look at both a 50-day and 200-day moving averages (and typically look at the interaction between the two to determine if the short-term average is higher or lower than the long-term average since that provides some information on relative trends in price – although I generally believe linear regression is a more effective way to make these determinations as will be discussed in more detail in a later chapter).

Chapter 13: Fundamental Evaluation of an Investment

As you can see, understanding the fundamental difference between price and value can be useful (and lucrative), when understood in the context of the U.S. economy. As you might also expect, this same analysis of the difference between price and value can be used for individual productive assets to determine whether or not purchasing any particular productive asset is a good idea, i.e. will pay a rate of return warranting the purchase price.

Price to Earnings and Price to Book

The first and most fundamental way to analyze an investment is by evaluating the purchase price by its residual income; that is to say its price to earnings. We have already encountered the mathematics of this evaluation in Chapter 8. For purposes here, we will discuss it in even more generic terms, but please feel free to refer back to the spreadsheet in Chapter 8.

Generally speaking, a productive assets income subtracted from its total costs (whether of operation, debt service, deferred purchase price, etc.) equals the productive assets net cash flow (i.e. the residual cash flow left over after the income has trickled through the waterfall of the capital structure). An equity investor in a productive asset is entitled to this net cash flow which represents the investor's return received in the form of income (i.e. this does not include any appreciative value in price).

To determine the rate of return relative to one's purchase price one takes the net cash flow and divides it by the purchase price. For real assets, this is referred to as the "capitalization rate" or "cap rate". There are many variations on the "cap rate" (mainly variations in omitting certain non-operational costs) and different uses, but at its most simple this indicates the proportion of net cashflow to purchase price. The higher this ratio, the more net cashflow (or productive ability) your asset has relative to the price you pay for such asset.

As already discussed, for public stock assets this is referred to as the "price to earnings" ratio (which is typically calculated on an earnings per share basis). That is to say, for public stocks one determines how much earnings each share is entitled to (by dividing the earnings by the number of outstanding shares) and then dividing the market price by this earnings per share figure. For the sake of completeness, earnings will be evidenced on the "Income Statement" for a public stock corporation, which will show net profit (the "bottom line" because of its physical position on the "Income Statement") after expenses are deducted from revenue (referred to often as the "top line" because of its physical position on the "Income Statement").

Because as we mentioned earlier, many purchases are financed with debt, it is also helpful to determine the rate of return on one's cash outlay. This is measured by dividing the net cashflow by the amount of cash utilized to purchase the asset. In a financed transaction, the cash on cash return should exceed the cap rate (because less cash is required to be used at the outset for the purchase). In a non-financed transaction, the cash on cash return will be the same as the cap rate (as the amount of cash used to purchase the productive asset will be the same as the purchase price). This is part of the reason, the interest of equity can diverge from debt interests on a productive asset. If we assume hypothetically, that an asset provides me with a cash on cash return of 50% annually and that to achieve such return I have financed 80% of the purchase price of the asset secured against that asset, after two years I will receive the full value of the cash I put into acquiring the asset and will consider myself "out" out of the asset. That is to say, I have no risk of losing the principal investment of cash I used to purchase the asset (whether or not this will be the case will largely be a result of two factors, mainly how much capital one has to contribute and how great a rate of return one can expect). Thus, after two years have passed, I may find myself less inclined to maintain the asset, as any return I receive after the two-year mark is in excess of my principal investment. Or, alternatively, I may be inclined to take additional risk, perhaps put on additional leverage (if possible), because if the asset defaults there is no recourse to me or risk of loss of my own principal investment and I would rather juice that excess return as much as possible.

In the context of public stocks, cash-on-cash return will take the form of "dividend yield". That is to say, most public stocks only pay out cash in the form of a dividend (if they pay out cash at all). Dividend yield will be roughly equivalent to cash-on-cash return in this context.

In our discussion above, we have been focusing on future cashflow to evidence value in a productive asset, but there are some assets which are difficult to value based on their cashflow. For these enterprises, looking at the value of the assets the asset holds is helpful in determining value. To put this in concrete terms, for financial firms (banks, asset managers, etc.), it is typically more helpful to look at their "price-to-book" ratio than their "price-to-earnings" ratio to get a sense of their real value. The calculation for "price-to-book" is similar to "price-to-earnings", that is to say you take the book value of the enterprise, divide it by the outstanding shares to get book value per share ("BVPS") and then take price and divide it by the BVPS. This will show you the price relative to the carrying value of the balance sheet of the enterprise.

Price-to-book is helpful for evaluating financial firms, because financial firms tend to own "financial assets", which are assets that are legal constructs, rather than physical assets. As an example, an investment bank is likely to have a "loan book" (which contains a ledger of all of the loans the bank has extended). This loan book will be updated continually with market prices (assuming the loans were given into a liquid market). So it will be quite readily possible to see the current market value of all underlying assets in the bank on a current basis. One can then evaluate the price relative to this "book value" to determine if an investor has to pay a premium over the financial assets the bank holds to purchase the bank, or less than the book value to purchase the bank. As we already know, if price is more than book, the bank is "overvalued" and if the price is less than book it is "undervalued" relative to the assets on its balance sheet. However, typically when banks are trading below book value, it is an indication that investors expect the loan book to perform poorly (or not at current market standards). Although this is speculative and may or may not be the case, it is a risk an investor runs if it buys at a price below book.

As you might expect, because financial institutions tend to hold "non-tangible" assets (that is to say they hold loan contracts and property rights on paper, but nothing physical typically), the financial footing of a financial institution is always more tenuous than an institution with real assets (like an industrial company). That is to say, one day the loan book could be fine, the next day you can wake up and the entire value of the banks has been haircut 25%. For an industrial company to endure the same loss would likely take months or even years, because the inherent value of physical assets takes time to erode (unlike contracts which can go from valuable to worthless as soon as they are breached). Additionally, because a bank can leverage their loan book, the addition of leverage can cause a financial institution to go insolvent quite quickly, if the loan book is risky and subject to rapid los in value.[52] This is also why financial institutions should always maintain a capital buffer (or liquidity buffer) to account for poor risk taking as well as limit the amount of leverage they are permitted to use[53].

---

[52] This was another contributor to the financial crisis of 2008, as banks leveraged their balance sheet heavily against assets which over the course of a few months turned out to be worthless. When these assets turned out to be worthless the creditors forced these institutions into insolvency and the financial institutions were then either bailed out by the federal government (i.e. the taxpayer) or allowed to be sold at pennies on the dollar to other banks to avoid a long and public bankruptcy proceeding.

[53] You don't want a systemically important financial institution betting the whole farm, because it will cause a lot of problems throughout the economy generally, since there are relatively few large financial institutions that provide credit to a lot of different industries, or said another way, systematically important financially institutions tend have their tentacles in everything one way or another, because of the concentration in the banking industry which has been permitted by world governments. Maintaining a capital buffer, however, causes a drag on return, because capital is stored for safety reasons and not used for productive purposes which would presumably generate return. As a result, the quantity and quality of the capital buffer that

It should also be noted that banks don't typically use their own money for their risk taking (that is to say to lend and to purchase investment assets), rather they take money from clients (who expect a return), from their depositaries (who also expect a return, albeit a much smaller one), and they have their own money (the bank's or proprietor's money) which they can invest. Thus, a bank (while you might not think of it that way), is really more of a conduit of money than anything. That is to say, they take other people's money (at a cost, known as the "cost of capital"), then lend it to other people (at an interest rate or price), and pocket the spread between these two.

As you might expect, the higher the cost of capital for investment, the more corresponding return will need to be taken to maintain the same spread as competitor banks. As a result, banks with high costs of capital tend to take more risk than banks with lower capital costs. Additionally, because banks tend to have departments which function within a slice of the market, in order to stay in their silo from a marketing perspective, banks with higher costs of capital will often attempt to be priced only slightly higher than others (and to take on more exotic deals) to preserve their spread, while not alienating their clients (and providing themselves with a market niche, since they would otherwise just be outpriced by competitors). As you might expect, this situation can become dangerous if the decision makers do not fully appreciate the risk of the loans being given (and such loans are being marketed as safer than they in fact are). That is to say, if you believe your loan is senior secured (and have

---

needs to be maintained is usually subject to much debate and a source of tension between financial institutions and their regulators.

priced it as such) and it is in fact not (even though superficially it appears senior secured), it is unlikely that you will be fairly compensated in return for the real risk of loss. To be clear, the issue is not necessarily that additional risk was taken for additional return, it is that the relative risk is not fully accounted for in the return generated (and often the fact that risk is often, at least in part, concealed and not known).

Additionally, it should be noted that even in banks where the cost of capital is not terribly high, because the decision maker has no real "skin in the game", the decision makers may be inclined to take risk that they otherwise shouldn't, because they do not fear the risk of loss. That is to say, most bankers get paid based on the volume of loans they give and at what spread (that is cost of capital to price of the loan, plus various fees). The larger the spread, the more money the banker will make (despite the larger relative risk probably being taken). The risk to the financial institution is that if the institution loses client money, the reputation of the firm may be so badly damaged that they may be ostracized by clients and go extinct.[54] Additionally, in a world where certain financial institutions are deemed "systemically" important and can rely on the prospect that the US government will step in and use taxpayer money to save them from poor decision making, there is an element of moral hazard, where bankers are

---

[54] Cynically my experience has been bankers on the ground tend not to care about the institution terribly because loans probably won't go bad until there is a recession and that will tend to be 10 years away generally, so they would rather be rich today and risk something bad that might happen to other people in the future, than to not get rich today, even if that means there may be negative repercussions to themselves.

encouraged to take outsized risk, to pad their own wallets, risking other people's money with the understanding that when everything fails the government will step in and save their institution anyway.

Generally speaking, risk and compliance officers at banks are supposed to step in and prevent the taking of excessive risk, but in practice, risk and compliance officers will often fail in this function.[55] To be clear, this is not to say that financial institutions or the individuals who work there are inherently good or bad, it is simply to say that the balance of risk, the culture and the general position of financial institutions in society (especially systemically important ones) tend to support, encourage and financially incentivize short-term profitably at the expense of long-term risk taking (which as we already discussed is the opposite asymmetry of risk that would be advisable for long-term sustainable investment success).[56]

---

[55] They often want to get paid too and killing deals doesn't get one a bonus. At other times they will be actively ignored, siloed or avoided, perhaps even fired.

[56] The general mindset appears to be that "no one will know who is swimming naked until the tide goes out", at which point one can hide in the crowd provided they are not engaged in the most obvious and extreme cases of poor or outlandish conduct. As it was explained to me by a senior banker, investment banking is like being a lineman in American football. Holding is going to occur on every play and provides a tactical advantage. Holding is not going to be caught and penalized on every play (and when penalized is penalized fairly minimally relative to the advantage provided), thus, it is most effective to hold on every play, provided you learn to do so in a way that leads you to get caught less often than the other linemen. Said another way, the risk analysis of many investment bankers and investment professionals is that doing the "wrong thing" is fine, provided it is done in a tactful, unobtrusive way, there are others doing the wrong thing in a more brazen way than you and provided the penalty for

Thus, while price-to-book is a helpful metric for analyzing certain enterprises (specifically financial organizations), for financial enterprises you can generally expect that the book value reported is inflated to some degree and more latent risk exist associated with the return expected from the book value than is anticipated. For this reason, it is usually a good idea to apply some sort of discount factor to the reported book value (to account for some level of additional risk of loss or overvaluing) when making an investment decision regarding a financial institution.

Variations of Calculating the Rate of Return

To be clear, despite the fact I have selected cap rate and cash on cash return as my chosen metrics of the rate of return, they are neither the only nor the most sophisticated calculations for determining one's rate of return (they are in fact the two simplest).

Two of the most common are Internal Rate of Return (or IRR) and Net Present Value (NPV), both of which are primarily concerned with the time preference of money and investments; that is to say both calculations are concerned with determining the value of all future cash flows of an investment in present value terms today. For IRR this creates an "effective interest rate" or "annualized

---

such conduct is not terribly severe relative to the benefits of such conduct. To be sure such a moral assessment of conduct based on the risk of being caught and the severity of punishment relative to the rewards resulting from such conduct is perfectly rational, albeit somewhat sociopathic and a slippery slope to rationalizing all kinds of socially detrimental activity. It is also, yet another example, of the herding behavior characteristic of poor financial risk takers in financial markets.

effective compounded return rate". For Net Present Value this will be expressed as a dollar figure (which should exceed 0 if the investment is to provide any monetary value). Generally speaking, both IRR and NPV, start with their base as the "cost of capital", that is to say what is the cost of using the capital that will be used to purchase the productive asset. For debt, that will be an interest rate. For equity, that will be an expected rate of return. The cost of capital is then weighted (based on what portion each is present). The future cash flows are then aggregated and "discounted" back to the present day (or measured what they would be in today's dollars, if you had all of the cash flow today). In NPV's case, the future cash flows (in present value terms) are subtracted from the principal capital to be invested (plus its weighted cost) to give you a dollar figure of the potential gain or loss resulting from investment. In IRR's case, the same calculation of future cash flows is performed, except the "spread" between the productive asset's nominal rate of return and the cost of capital is provided as the "effective interest rate" one can expect on one's capital from investing in the productive asset (rather than calculating out the dollar figure).

Generally speaking, NPV is a more accurate reflection of the value of future cash flows, but IRR is typically preferred by investment professionals because it is easier to compare IRR since it is expressed on a percentage basis (and is therefore easier to compare across investments which vary in size, since size weighting is removed). IRR is the preferred method of evaluating private equity returns in most cases. It should also be noted that both equations can be manipulated (IRR more significantly), by unscrupulous investment professionals wishing to market themselves as producing a greater return than they in fact do (typically by taking measures to adjust costs of capital or by varying discount factors). For this reason, it is important to always consider one's cash on cash return (to ensure you are receiving the value you expect to receive, despite someone's reporting of a high IRR).[57]

---

[57] One way, investment professionals accomplish this is something known as the "Subscription-Commitment Facility" or "SCF". An "SCF" is a loan given by a bank to a fund manager, in which the pledged collateral is the contractual right to call the capital committed by the funds investors (that is to say, its collateral is a non-tangible contractual right to underlying property). The idea from the lender's perspective is that if the investors in the fund are creditworthy institutions it is a safe bet that they will have capital (even in a distressed scenario) to fund the total value of the principal of the loans (and if the fund performs well they get the benefit of receiving cashflow from the fund's positive performance in the form of an interest rate or said another way having "exposure" to the fund's investments). From the fund's perspective, taking out a loan on the capital committed to the fund rather than just using the investor capital, has the beneficial effect of lowering the fund's "weighted average cost of capital" or "WACC" because the cost of capital on a loan is typically less than the cost of capital from investors (that is to say the bank demands an interest rate at a senior secured level in the risk continuum which has a correspondingly low interest rate relative to the high return equity investors require for the benefit of using their capital). Similarly, delaying a capital call from investors using leverage has a time value of money benefit, since the less time that transpires between when investor capital is allocated and the return is attained, the greater the IRR. Said simply, because the fund takes a loan out against the promise of its investors to provide cash for investment, rather than asking the investors to give the fund that cash and investing it directly, the IRR of the fund will be higher than a fund who has the exact same investment return, but instead uses the capital of its investors to invest. Having a high IRR, is then marketed as "market beating" or "outperformance" and typically makes fundraising additional capital in the future for a new fund easier. Additionally, most funds typically have a "hurdle rate" or a rate of return which must be achieved before the fund manager can share in the profit of the fund (called "carried interest"). Using an SCF to juice

DuPont analysis is yet another model for measuring one's Return on Investment (or "ROI"), although its utility is beyond the scope of this book other than to say, it operates by analyzing one's return using a series of ratios based on profitability, asset efficiency and the use of financial leverage (and can be used as an effective barometer in some industries for measuring whether management is operating a productive asset in a healthy and efficient manner).

---

the IRR can, in some cases, help the fund manager to reach the hurdle rate.

Similarly, once investments are purchased for the fund, funds tend to place leverage directly on the acquired assets since it has the effect of deferring the purchase price of those assets (and placing the burden of paying off this leverage on the purchased asset itself) thereby increasing rate of return (if done correctly this has a beneficial effect on both the IRR and cash on cash return as discussed earlier), although depending on the amount of asset level leverage, can make the fund vulnerable to distress events in the underlying pool of assets that the fund owns. This asset level leverage strategy also tends to incentivize leaving underperforming assets for dead, rather than try to manage them through a distress event, since an asset imploding under its own debt load, probably won't expose the fund to any risk of principal loss and abandoning the asset may be enough to minimize the effect of damaging the rate of return to the fund, especially if the fund enjoyed a period of time at rate of return, with the benefit of that leverage, sufficient to extract a suitable rate of return from the asset before it failed).

To be fair, however, it is important to mention that SCFs do have a practical functional benefit, mainly preventing short-term liquidity issues for a fund and serving as a sort of bridge loan that allows managers to react quickly when deals become available (allowing a manager to purchase an asset when it becomes available on the market rather than needing to wait for capital to be called from investors to make the purchase).

Risk of Loss and Risk Adjusted Return

After determining the rate of return, the next important factor in determining whether an asset is a good investment on a fundamental basis, is to determine the risk associated with achieving that rate of return.

There are two primary risks associated with any productive asset: 1) the loss of the principal amount of capital required to invest (i.e. the purchase price or the amount of capital contributed to the purchase price; and 2) the certainty of the future cash flow. One can think of these two risks as the two inherent risks of the capital structure, first, security of the rights to the underlying productive asset in accordance with the continuum of risk (priority in right) and second, the rights to priority of payment in the capital structure (as cashflow trickles down the waterfall) (priority in payment).

Risk of Loss of Principal

The risk of loss of principal, in equity terms, is the risk that you lose the capital you invested to purchase the asset (or contributed toward the purchase of the asset), in debt terms, this is the risk you lose the principal amount of the loan you extended. The risk of loss is measured in various ways depending on the type of asset, but generally speaking, falls into the continuum of risk expressed in Chapter 10. That is to say, the risk of loss is largely dependent on whether you will have any recourse to remaining assets if cashflow is distressed (i.e. if you are secured against assets) or if your return is great enough that you will receive return sufficient to recoup your investment within a short-time period.

The risk of loss of principal is largely a result of the following four factors: 1) whether the asset is solvent, 2) whether the asset is liquid, 3) whether the investor has any rights in collateral in the event of insolvency, and 4) whether there is any residual or retained value in the underlying asset in a distressed scenario.

1) Solvency

Solvency is a measure of a productive assets ability to pay off its debt obligations. That is to say, it is a measure of whether or not there are enough assets to pay off all financial obligations. If a company has more debt than it has asset value then it is considered to be "insolvent". In the case of insolvency, lenders can typically force a debtor into a legal proceeding known as "bankruptcy", which involves the orderly sale of assets, overseen by the law (typically a "trustee" or "administrator"), to prioritize the payment of debt in order of such debt's priority and to maximize any residual asset value realized through liquidation (i.e. by selling off assets). Typically, secured creditors are also entitled to seek recourse outside of bankruptcy, including foreclosing on assets (i.e. seizing assets) in which the lender has a secured interest (known as "collateral" for the secured loan). Whether or not foreclosure can occur outside of bankruptcy is a matter of law and varies by jurisdiction.

To measure the solvency of an enterprise, one can use the solvency ratio, also called the debt-to-assets ratio. The debt-to-assets ratio is calculated by dividing the total liabilities of an enterprise by total assets. One can also look to the debt-to-equity ratio (which will tell you largely the same thing as the debt-to-assets ratio, because it simply uses the only other element of the balance sheet, which by definition must be proportional). It is calculated by dividing the total debt by the total equity.

To measure whether an enterprise will be able to service its debt in a given period one uses the interest coverage ratio. The interest coverage ratio is calculated by dividing a company's earnings before interest and taxes by the company's interest expenses for that period. This calculation, thereby, measures the margin of safety an asset has for paying interest on its debt for a given period. That is to say, how many times earnings earned can cover the debt service or "cost of debt", i.e. the interest (which contributed to those earnings). It is for this reason that it is sometimes referred to as "times interest earned". Lenders and creditors tend to use this formula to determine if the company has sufficient earnings to cover the cost of its excising debt or can afford to take on additional debt. The danger of course to relying solely on an interest coverage ratio, is that earnings will tend to increase as additional debt is taken on (since short term buying power has been increased by borrowing and presumably used to acquire or contribute to an asset that produces earnings). Thus, initially, additional earnings will encourage additional lending, which will encourage additional earnings, which in turn will encourage additional lending. This will continue to increase (if one ignores other ratios), until an unhealthy amount of leverage has been placed on an asset. When that asset, enters a slowing or decay phase (typically at the end of the growth cycle), the debt will often prove to be unsustainable. That is to say, there will be insufficient earnings, to pay debt service or the cost debt (which could happen quite suddenly depending on the rate of decay in earnings). When this happens, an otherwise healthy asset, which otherwise appears fine, could end up insolvent because its debt load is more than its equilibrium earnings can afford (despite the fact the whole way up the growth curve it appeared healthy).[58]

A similar, but slightly more comprehensive ratio is called the "debt service coverage ratio". It is calculated by taking net operating income (which is generally considered EBIT as in times interest earned) and dividing it by the total debt service. Total debt service is slightly more comprehensive than interest expense, because it includes both the interest and principal on a debt due for a particular period. For many financial assets (which are designed to always carry an amount of leverage on a productive asset), debt service coverage will be the same mathematically as interest coverage because principal on such assets tends to be due as a "balloon payment at maturity". That is to say, the principal is never due, until the loan ends (at which point it is typically refinanced into a new loan or "rolled over" and never paid off in the entire life of the productive asset). However, for an amortizing loan, like a common mortgage, the debt service coverage ratio will be more comprehensive than interest coverage, because it will include the amount of principal due in the denominator. In any case, debt service coverage is designed to tell you largely the same information as interest coverage, that is to

---

[58] Usually during this time, management will take steps to try and preserve earnings, which usually will take the form of "cost cutting" measures. That is to say, mathematically, to produce more earnings you can either increase revenue or decrease costs. As you might expect, this tends to effect employees, because employees are usually the most expensive cost to a business, so you tend to see layoffs right before an enterprise starts to truly struggle. Additionally, cutting costs (depending on whether this is done effectively or ineffectively) tends to hamper growth (because you have less people to produce revenue), and is usually a sign that an enterprise is slowing into a decay phase.

say, are earnings (cashflow) sufficient to cover the payments for a borrowing.

It is important to note that the data for the first two ratios (the debt-to-assets and debt-to-equity ratios) were sourced from information contained on the balance sheet, whereas the second two ratios (interest coverage ratio and debt service coverage ratio) are sourced from information contained on the income statement. Generally speaking, while the income statement is important for determining future cash flows and ongoing expenses, the balance sheet is really the best place to determine the overall health of an organization.[59]

2) Liquidity

Liquidity is the ability of a productive assets ability to pay off its "current liabilities" from its "current assets". Generally speaking, "current liabilities" are financial obligations that are due in a year or less and "current assets" are assets which can be converted to cash (or cash equivalents) within a year. Thus, liquidity is the ability of an asset to pay off its short-term debt using short-term assets.

Liquidity is important because even if the long-term solvency of an asset is healthy, if an asset cannot pay its short-term obligations using short-term assets, it will default on these short-term obligations and can be forced into insolvency. (Lender's typically have a right to accelerate a loan, make a claim of default, and seize collateral if you miss a short-term debt payment or if you generally default on a short-term obligation, even if such

---

[59] Many an investor has ignored the balance sheet in favor of the income statement at their own peril.

default is only because you don't have the cash today, despite the fact you may have sufficient long-term assets in excess of total liabilities and are otherwise a healthy enterprise). Such an event, can force an otherwise solvent creditor into insolvency. The main ratios for liquidity include the current ratio, quick ratio and cash ratio.

The current ratio is calculated by dividing "current assets" by "current liabilities". If this ratio is greater than one, the enterprise has the capital on hand to meet short-term obligations. If the ratio is less than one, the enterprise does not have the capital on hand to meet short-term obligations and therefore cannot cover all of its current debts. It is important to note, however, that because cashflow to an enterprise is not always "smooth", to effectively use the current ratio, one needs to look at such ratio for more than a single time period. (Generally speaking, corporations smooth out volatility in cash flow using short-term debt called "commercial paper" or longer-term revolving loans, which are effectively lines of credit similar to credit cards, provided they are solvent enough to take on such debt).

The quick ratio (sometimes called the "acid test" ratio) is calculated by aggregating cash and cash equivalents with marketable securities and accounts receivable and then dividing this sum by the current liabilities. In accounting speak, it is generally the same as the current ratio, except it doesn't include the common current assets of "inventory" and "prepaid expense" because inventory and prepaid expense cannot be readily turned into cash in the short term (within 90 days or so). The quick ratio therefore measures the amount of liquid assets an enterprise has to pay off its current liabilities (within a 90 day billing period as opposed to within a year). Generally speaking, a quick ratio of 1 means an enterprise has the liquid assets to pay its short-term obligations (although accounts receivable have a rate of collection and often needs to be discounted based on how much accounts receivable can reasonably be expected to be collected in the period).

The cash ratio is calculated by aggregating cash and cash equivalents and then dividing this sum by the current liabilities. As you can probably tell, this is the same as the quick ratio, without accounts receivable and marketable securities and is therefore the most conservative of the ratios listed. The cash ratio is a measure of an enterprise's ability to repay its short-term debt with readily liquid resources. The cash ratio tends to be the most commonly used metric for liquidity, because it tells you readily whether an organization is able to pay all of its current liabilities if forced to do so immediately (after all it's all fun and games in the world of mathematical ratios until you need the cash and you can't come up with it). Once again, a ratio of 1, indicates an organization has the cash to pay off its short-term debt.

All of the liquidity ratios discussed are all based on information found on an organization's balance sheet. As already mentioned, the balance sheet typically has the information necessary to determine the overall health of an organization.

3) Priority of Rights in Collateral

Generally speaking, the priority of right of claims to residual asset value follows the risk continuum set forth in Chapter 10. That is to say, senior secured creditors are prioritized first (and typically are given first priority rights in the assets to which they have been assigned collateral interests). Junior secured creditors are prioritized second. Senior creditors who are unsecured are prioritized next (even though they have no rights in collateral, they have a senior right in payment in liquidation proceedings). Junior unsecured creditors are next. Mezzanine and any hybrid debt are prioritized next (absent a subordination agreement which would give a higher priority in right to warrants or the like). Preferred equity is then prioritized. Finally, any remaining residual value is returned to the equity holders (although in insolvency by definition there are insufficient asset value to provide any residual value to the equity holders).

To be clear, debt (the obligation to return money borrowed) is a contractual right that can be secured by the granting of a security interest which provides for the assignment of property rights in certain designated assets (known as "collateral") through a process known in the U.S. as "attachment" (i.e. the collateral property right is attached to the contractual right to repay debt). In order to ensure the priority of one's attachment to such collateral is above all others, a security interest is typically required to be "perfected". That is to say, a legal process is required (which varies based on the type of asset, type of claim and the jurisdiction in which the security interest, as a property right, is granted), which typically requires some sort of notice requirement (to put other lenders or claimants on notice of your claim) and/or filing in a centralized registry (so future claimants can see that you have a right that would be superior to their claim). Absent a "perfected" interest, the law typically defaults to a first-in-time, first-in-right method for priority to settle disputes between two or more claims over the same collateral with the same priority.

Assuming a security interest is properly attached and recorded, a property right is created for the benefit of the lender (in what would otherwise be the borrower's asset) senior to all other claims. (It is notable, however, that this priority can be contracted away through use of a "subordination agreement" or "intercreditor agreement" setting forth the priority to which creditors agree to be subject in terms of order of priority).

Conversely, if debt is unsecured, it is merely a contractual right, which depending on the contracted for priority in payment (which again can be contracted for among other creditors through intercreditor or subordination agreements), places the creditor in line in a judicial proceeding to receive residual value from any remaining assets after secured claims are met.

Equity will have a residual right in whatever property is left over after secured creditors have seized whatever collateral is necessary to be made whole, and contractual creditors have received any residual asset value necessary to make them whole (in an insolvency scenario there would by definition be no remaining value, although in a liquidity scenario there may be assets left over for equity, although this tends not to be the case). Preferred equity will rank above common equity in priority of payment, but generally speaking, neither can expect to receive much value relative to their principal investment of capital from residual value remaining after the creditors have been fully satisfied.

To be clear, a secured claim has a property interest in the underlying asset of value provided the security interest is properly attached and perfected (which is largely a mechanical legal process of properly documenting the attachment and perfecting through notice and recordation).

However, despite being properly attached and perfected, there is a latent danger that can potentially arise in what otherwise appears superficially as a senior secured right to collateral. This latent danger is called "structural subordination".

A senior secured claim which is otherwise properly attached and perfected could potentially be subject to subordination to other more senior claims (without having contracted to be subordinated or otherwise being aware that it has been subordinated), if such claim is "structurally subordinated" to another claim. That is to say, in complex financial structures, an asset may be owned by a holding company which itself contains no assets other than the underlying asset it holds. The underlying asset may be indebted with senior secured claims against this underlying asset. The holding company's common equity (which as we know is a right to control the holding company and its assets and to receive residual cash flow) may then also be pledged as collateral for a loan at the holding company level. At the holding company level, this would be considered a "senior secured claim" to the equity in the holding company (since no claimant ranks higher or has a secured right to the equity in the holding company). However, as a practical matter, the ability to receive any residual value in the underlying asset in an insolvency scenario is significantly impaired because such senior secured debt at the holding company level ranks behind the

4) Residual or Retention of Value

From a risk perspective, the main point here is that in order to feel secure that the capital contributed as principal will be recouped in a distress scenario, one must be confident that there is residual value in the underlying asset in such distressed scenario sufficient to recoup such principal invested.

For senior secured creditors, property rights in collateral ensure that a creditor receives some residual value in the underlying asset. If the lenders have appropriately evaluated the portfolio and appropriately secured and perfected their rights in adequate collateral (typically the entire pool of assets in a portfolio), then the senior secured creditor should be fairly comfortable that in an insolvency scenario, the senior secured creditor will recoup the full value of their principal. That is to say, three factors determine, whether a lender will recover the principal of their loan in insolvency 1) proper security of interests, 2) priority of ranking in the security and 3) the amount of value the loan was secured against. If 1 and 2 are satisfied, the only question is whether a sufficient amount of collateral was pledged. Generally, for a diversified portfolio of assets, a senior secured creditor should be comfortable if a loan is equal to approximately 50% of the value of the portfolio. That is to say the "loan to value" ratio (the lent amount divided by the total portfolio value) is 50%.

The reason for this 50% benchmark, is because a properly diversified portfolio should only sustain a 50%

---

environment, that has largely eroded the standards for investment grade debt.

decline in a period of total economic distress (i.e. a major recession on a whole economy scale). In such a scenario, the bank will step in recoup the entire value of their loan, the equity will walk away with nothing (but may not care because they may have received a return in excess of the value of the portfolio over the expansionary years) and the lenders who are not senior secured will generally get no recovery (other than what they received in interest, which was likely not sufficient to recover the value of their principal). If a more than 50% decline is sustained, the senior secured debt will recoup less then their principal, but will be generally comfortable that they are no worse off than every other investment banking group, since generally investment banks tend to use the same metrics (and tend to do things in crowds since it is viewed as safer from a policy perspective, since the outlier tends to get sanctioned for being too risky and the employees tend to be evaluated based on their performance relative to other employees). If you are paying close attention you will recognize this behavior as mimetic as well (which exacerbates the debt cycle issues described earlier), since most creditors seem to desire to take the same risks in the same industries on the basis of perceived safety (which tends to exacerbate destruction of value during decay phases, as bankers attempt to flee the carnage or seek recourse at the same time).[61]

As you might expect, recovery sufficient to protect a senior secured creditor's principal investment in this scenario is subject to the residual value which is available to be recouped. That is to say, there are two latent dangers

[61] In a herding paradigm, not unlike the one which tends to plague analysts and economists.

in the property right of a senior secured lender in collateral: 1) whether there is sufficient value in a distressed scenario in the collateral and 2) to what the property right in collateral entitles the holder.

Looking back for a moment at our 50% LTV rule, it doesn't take much to see that if the residual value of the collateral falls below 50%, then there will be insufficient collateral to cover the principal loan investment.[62] This tends to occur when investors or lenders don't fully understand the risk of the portfolio of assets. That is to say, the portfolio is perceived as diversified but is not, or is perceived hedged but is not (or generally there is some residual safety mechanism perceived that does not in fact materialize). Generally speaking, for a senior secured lender (who is and should be relying on the ability to recoup value), it is important to have comfort that the residual value of the collateral exceeds the principal

---

[62] For ease the example assumes that none of the principal of the loan is paid off during the life of the loan (that is to say the loan does not amortize and the principal is due as a balloon payment at maturity). If there is an amortizing component, the amount of time that passes before the loan becomes distressed is highly relevant, because as time goes on a portion of principal is recouped (that is to say the lender is racing the clock to some degree). If the loan is amortizing and has been performing well prior to default for a length of time, it may not be tremendously detrimental if the collateral falls below the 50% of its value, because in the time before the distress occurred the lender will have collected back some of the principal investment. At this point, the lender would need to calculate the amount of principal left to be paid and compare that to the amount of collateral value remaining. Because this complicates the example above, we will ignore this for now for the sake of ease, but it is important to be aware of such a scenario, because an amortizing loan has a different risk to principal than a balloon payment (and the modeling for each from a risk-return perspective is different).

amount of the loan. Typically this is calculated as a "recovery rate" (or its inverse the "loss given default" rate) and is an important risk metric to consider on senior secured debt (and debt generally). Generally speaking, the recovery rate is the amount of principal and accrued interest (i.e. interest earned but unpaid) that can be expected to be recovered in a default scenario. The loss given default (LGD) is the inverse of the recovery rate, that is to say, the amount of loss expected on principal and accrued interest in the event of default. As you might expect, as you move down the continuum of risk the recovery rate decreases as risk increases and return should correspondingly increase to compensate for the increase in the LGD.

The second latent danger of the sufficiency of collateral is the nature of the property right received. That is to say, a senior secured claim which is otherwise properly attached and perfected could potentially have the value of its property interest eroded because of the nature of the property secured as collateral. To be clear, here we are not referring to one's collateral interest being eroded because of a lack of residual value, but rather we are suggesting that there is a deficiency in the claim to such collateral. This tends to happen in more sophisticated instruments where derivatives, contractual claims, or other "non-tangible assets" (typically contractual rights to real assets) are the pledged "collateral" for loans.

As we have already stated, the benefit of senior security is that it creates a "property right" in something of value. However, if our "collateral" i.e., the item of value, is not a real asset, what we actually have is a property right in a contractual right to some property. As you might expect, adding this contractual interloper between the property right and the real asset, can cause a variety of issues. The first and most significant of which is that a contractual claim, under the law, is not as secure as a property right. If I have a property right, something of tangible value belongs to me. If I have a property right in something non-tangible, the property right I have is something of value that is derivative to performance of something else of tangible value. That is to say, my access to the actual item of value is impeded by my need to enforce performance of a contractual right.

Financially minded individuals tend to like to create derivatives and non-tangible asset rights/contractual rights, because there can be many more derivatives and contractual rights than there can ever be real assets. That is to say, using contracts and derivatives, I can create a new asset of perceived value, without actually having to create anything of real tangible value. As an example, if I have a house, I can break up the value of my house into a bunch of contractual rights to receive various benefits from the use of the house (or "derivative" rights), all of which are underpinned by the real asset. I can then take this second layer of "derivative" contractual rights and ask a bank to give me a loan with these "derivative" contractual rights as the collateral, which by law creates a property right in the derivative contracts. As you can see from this example, there is only ever one house, but I can effectively create additional property out of nothing by making agreements with others for various rights or performance and recharacterizing these contractual rights as property. Additionally, if I am the lender in this scenario, the collateral is a level away from anything of real value which I could hope to seize. When I foreclose, I just get a piece of paper that says I'm entitled to something else, but I still need to try and enforce contractually on this piece of paper (which may or not be possible).

If this sounds complicated to you that is because it is and is in fact designed to be. The important thing to note here, is that there is only one underlying real productive asset of value and all of the contractual and property rights layered on top of it are inherently tied to the same performance of that underlying real asset. Each layer of rights, however, create an additional set of assets (basically out of thin air), which allows an additional layer of fees to the financial professionals and the potential for an additional layer of leverage.

It should also be noted that because contract rights are private rights and the law generally prioritizes "freedom of contract". Contract law is more or less the "Wild West" of legal theory. Almost anything goes, provided it would not erode the moral fabric of society (that is to say, I can't legally contract to have someone killed), but generally speaking there is a lot of leeway for parties to contract. Property rights (because property and real assets suffer from scarcity of resources) are more rigid and real assets cannot be created simply by drawing up paper (they exist in the real world and must be sourced or built in a more organic fashion).

As you might expect, the more derivatives, contracts and legal structures piled on to the same pool of assets the more leverage is likely associated with that same underlying asset and the greater the risk of default to everyone up the chain if the underlying asset underperforms. Additionally, because investors up the chain tend to realize having an interest in non-tangible assets is dangerous, they tend to package them together into "diversified" bundles and resell them as "safe". The end result of this is typically a mispricing of risk, an additional generated fee for the structurer, and a greater risk of "contagion" across industries, as investors find out they have exposure to underlying assets to which they didn't realize they had an association (which has a negative impact on whatever industry they are engaged in primarily).

Taking a step back for a moment however, on a small scale, being just one contractual layer away from an underlying asset is more dangerous from a collateral perspective than if the same lender has a property right in that asset itself. This should make intuitive sense. If I have a property right to a parcel of land, and the borrower doesn't pay I can go take that house. If I have a property right to a contract to sell me a parcel of land, if a borrower defaults, as a lender I have a property right to step into the shoes of the party to that contract and demand that the contract be enforced (mainly that I be given the right to purchase the land). Whether or not I will actually be able to purchase the land could be contested under contract law and I may need to go to court to enforce at which point a court could decide (after seeing the "totality of the evidence") that perhaps that contract is unenforceable. Even if the contract is enforceable, receiving my collateral will most certainly take longer and be less certain (courts tend to favor monetary settlements over specific performance in any case since it is less socially disruptive). The more layers I add, the less certain my recovery and the greater my LGD (even though it may and often will be marketed as "safe" and "senior secured").

To be clear, this is not a moral judgment on derivatives and their use. I, personally, enjoy derivatives. I find them useful for hedging certain risk and to increase return (particularly when trading over short-time horizons). I have personally seen their utility in the energy sector for mitigating potential losses resulting from potential price swings in underlying commodity prices used to power energy generating facilities. The point rather is that when used as collateral for a loan, by its very nature non-tangible collateral is inherently riskier than tangible collateral, and as such requires compensation in the form of additional return. It can also be dangerous to investors if the risk lurks latently and investors don't properly account for this risk in making capital allocations (most of the time because they don't realize the risk exists). As you might expect, not accounting for risk tends to negatively impact the "risk-adjusted return" on these investments (that is to say, the risk of loss tends to be greater than accounted for in the expected return).

Generally speaking, however, because senior secured creditors tend to get back their principal investment and equity tends to get return in excess of their investment, it usually makes the most sense to be either a senior secured creditor or to be equity as an investor, while being in the middle of the capital structure is most likely to lead to loss (or at minimum risk-adjusted underperformance). Investors who are invested in junior or subordinated debt tend to suffer the worst risk-adjusted performance over time because in times of distress they frequently believe themselves to be secured even though they aren't (or aren't fully) and the returns generated prior to the distress are insufficient to account for the principal loss. Said another way, the risk associated with the middle of the capital structure tends to not generate enough return to warrant the risk taken.

Also, interesting is that investors, who believe themselves to be sophisticated, tend to desire to take the "middle ground" because they want to receive out-performance while still retaining "adequate" security. Unfortunately, doing both effectively is extremely difficult to achieve. As a result, it typically is more effective to be either hot or cold, rather than being lukewarm and getting spat out. Said in more financial terms, in times of distress investors in the middle of the capital structure tend to get the poorest "risk-adjusted return" (although superficially they may appear to be in a better position than equity).

Conversely, a strategy with exposure at both ends of the capital structure rather than the middle (while perhaps not immediately obvious) tends to perform better on a "risk-adjusted" basis. I generally refer this as a "barbell strategy". That is to say having a collection of super safe and super high-risk investments from a capital structure continuum perspective (i.e. risk-free or senior secured debt on one end and common equity on the other) tends to generate superior risk-adjusted returns, relative to having a selection of a basket of assets throughout the capital structure.

The main value of this "barbell strategy" is that mathematically it provides an average return equivalent to being somewhere in the middle of the risk continuum, but minimizes the loss of invested principal. If you think about it this should make some intuitive sense since only assets on the far sides of the risk continuum are "property rights" as opposed to contractual rights. That is to say senior secured debt has a right in the productive asset sufficient to account for the principal allocated in a distressed scenario (if the collateral is priced properly) and the equity has the property right in all residual cash flow (which should provide the best return from the productive asset in cashflow terms and should exceed the principal amount invested over the growth phase of the productive asset). Everyone in the middle of the capital structure is just a contractual claim to some share of cash flow in proportion of increasing risk of loss in exchange for providing capital to the borrower.

The exception to this of course is when the senior secured creditor's collateral has a latent danger, mainly, its rights in collateral are deficient or its access to collateral value is insufficient. As already discussed these latent dangers typically result because of opaque and overly complex financial structures (mostly designed to generate fees for those who create them and generate outsized returns by over-leveraging the equity that sponsors them). Generally speaking, when senior secured collateral is structurally subordinated in such a way that it actual becomes junior debt or when the senior secured collateral is a contractual right (that is to say the property right is in an asset that is non-tangible or contractual in nature), the return is most likely insufficient to compensate for the latent risk of loss and it should be avoided. Instinctively, such a structure, probably seems a bit perverse in any case because it is designed to undermine the value of being a senior secured creditor in the first place (because at that level in the capital structure you sacrifice higher returns for the sake of safety of one's principal). Once again, this is not to say that structural subordination or non-tangible collateral is inherently bad. It is just that doing either of these things moves one down the risk continuum (even if

To be clear, this is inherently backward looking (and past performance is no guarantee of future returns as we've previously seen), but it is more or less the best that can be calculated. Additionally, one can fairly accurately speculate on the certainty of future cashflow by taking a general view of the typical life-cycle of a particular type of productive asset, since cashflow tends to increase or decrease with the productive life of an asset (like the cells in the lab) and a longer productive life will tend to result in cashflow over a longer period of time (provided no disruptive technology disrupts such growth). As also mentioned earlier, cashflow also tends to be subject to the debt cycles overlaid on top of the growth cycles.

Risk-Adjusted Return

Together the opportunity cost of the loss of future expected cash flow and the loss of invested principal comprises the "risk" of an investment. As we have already discussed, for any risk taken above "risk-free", we expect to receive a premium of return above the "risk-free rate" in proportion to the additional risk undertaken. As such, the better the rate of return relative to the risk of loss the better an investment is considered. This is referred to as the "risk-adjusted return" or the return measured by the amount of risk which was involved in producing such return.

There are a number of ways to calculate/evaluate risk-adjusted return, but for our purposes, the most common measures for the risk-adjusted return for a portfolio of productive assets are R-squared, standard deviation and the Sharpe ratio. By way of brief explanation, R-squared is a measure of the variance a data set has from an index or benchmark (that is to say how well your portfolio tracks an index); standard deviation is the dispersion of a dataset relative to its mean (or said another way a measure of the volatility in the return of an asset relative to the average return); and the Sharpe ratio is the return subtracting the risk-free rate divided by the standard deviation of the excess return of the portfolio (or said another way the return after discounting the risk-free return divided by the volatility of such return). Of these, the Sharpe Ratio (or variants thereof) is probably the most widely used in evaluating a portfolio (and forms the basis of understanding of diversification generally), as it has the effect of measuring the return earned in excess of the risk-free rate per unit of volatility from a portfolio.

As you can see, the Sharpe Ratio has the effect of incorporating the factors of risk we were describing earlier, that is to say, it discounts the risk-free rate from the returns generated by the productive asset (since only returns received over the risk-free rate can be considered premium compensating us for the risk of potentially losing our principal) and then compares it to the volatility of the productive asset from its average return (that is to say how consistent is its return over time).

Generally, speaking the more return a portfolio of assets generates relative to the amount of risk taken, the better the "risk-adjusted return". That is to say, generally speaking, receiving more return at less risk is superior than receiving the same return, but having greater risk of loss.

There are only a few effective ways to reduce risk of loss (and in general investors tend to be fairly poor at effectively implementing these measures), since generally speaking risk and return are correlated (risk and return are in fact correlated by their very nature because additional return is intended to compensate investors for taking additional risk over the risk-free rate). These methods of reducing risk of loss and thereby increasing "risk-adjusted" returns are: 1) diversification, 2) hedging/insurance, 3) allocation of capital structure exposure, 4) market timing, 5) indexing/cost reduction and 6) the barbell strategy.

Chapter 14: Strategies for Mitigating the Continuum of Risk and Increasing Risk-Adjusted Returns

As mentioned in the prior chapter, there are a number of strategies which should theoretically reduce the risk of loss (both principal loss and loss of expected future returns) regardless of one's place on the risk-continuum. That is to say, the strategies listed below, are designed to boost risk-adjusted premium, by reducing risk without sacrificing return (or only marginally giving up return).

1) Diversification

The first and perhaps most commonly used and recognizable strategy is diversification. Diversification is a process by which assets with the same (or near same rate of return) and therefore similar risk profiles, but whose underlying risks are not correlated, are purchased. The idea behind diversification is based on probability. That is to say, it is generally believed that it is unlikely that risks which are uncorrelated to one another will all occur at the same time. Based on this logic, if one asset fails to perform, the damage caused by such failure will be minimized because the remaining assets (which are not correlated to that asset) will continue to perform. Said another way, if the return stays the same, but the risk is spread across multiple assets with uncorrelated risk, the risk-adjusted rate of return will be higher (because the same return is achieved with less risk).

The key as you might have noticed is that in order for diversification to work, the underlying risk of each asset cannot be correlated. If they are correlated, then purchasing the additional asset doesn't effectively minimize risk because these assets will tend to under-perform at the same time.

The main mathematical benefit of diversification is that if done correctly it decreases the probability of risk of loss, diminishes the magnitude of potential loss and thereby diminishes the potential for decreases in the expected rate of return. Said another way, it diminishes risk of loss without affecting the rate of return (and therefore without adjusting positioning in the risk continuum). The other practical benefit of diversification is that it is fairly easy to understand conceptually (although it can be surprisingly difficult to implement correctly).

By way of example, if you have an asset that returns 10% annually, your risk-adjusted return will be inferior to a portfolio of 15 assets (none of which are correlated with one another) that returns 10%. The portfolio of 15 assets is superior, even though the return is the same, because the risk of loss is reduced by the diversification.

The danger of diversification of course is if it is done improperly. That is to say, it is typically fairly difficult to find assets with the same rate of return that aren't in some way correlated. Using the equity markets as an example, most public stocks will generally be correlated with the overall market and one-another. Stocks that do not follow the market, tend to be "inversely correlated" (or "defensive") and tend to perform well when the broader market is underperforming. Said another way, it is difficult to find uncorrelated stocks that all perform well at the same time (at a similar rate of return). It is more likely that you will find uncorrelated stocks whose returns are also not correlated, which will drag the performance of the portfolio down (since during positive broad market times, it will not receive the full return, because an asset in the portfolio will be underperforming), although during broad market downturns, the portfolio will enjoy the benefit of increased return. Over-time this tends to result in simply "market returns" despite the extra effort to diversify.

While my example of inverse correlation was a bit extreme, in practice, there tends to be a continuum of correlation among risk assets (particularly in the equity markets), which can be effectively selected to reduce risk. The danger I am seeking to highlight is that such diversification (if the portfolio is large enough and diversified enough) tends to perform no better than an index of the broader market.

Also, quite typically, people don't understand that to be properly diversified, there must not be correlation of assets, so many investors buy a selection of risk assets that have a similar return, but are correlated (although they often do not realize it). As a result they tend to suffer greater loss during broad market downturns than they expect to or should if they properly diversified.

In passing, I would also just mention that diversification tends to have no real value in value investing, since each investment, in true value investing, should be invested in on the basis of its own merit and should have a value proposition relative to its price, such that another form of portfolio protection is not truly necessary. I will also mention, however, that while value investing should generally out-perform the broader market, if a portfolio of "value investing" assets becomes large enough, it will eventually begin to track the benchmarks. We will discuss this is in more depth in the next chapter.

Before we move on, I should reiterate that the type of diversification we have been discussing occurs within the same level of the risk continuum (that is to say within the same type of risk assets or "asset class"). Diversification across the risk continuum/capital structure, is a different strategy (since return fluctuates as well), which for purposes of clarity I have termed "allocation of capital structure exposure" and will be discussed separately below.[65]

2) Allocation of Capital Structure Exposure

Another common strategy for reducing the risk of loss is to spread one's capital across the risk continuum, or said another way, to allocate investment across the capital structure. The risk continuum is a continuum of both risk and return, thus as you start at the top of the risk continuum your return is low but your risk is also low. As you travel down the risk continuum your return becomes high but your risk becomes high as well.

As you might expect if you allocate capital across the capital structure, you decrease your risk and your return from the return of common equity (the riskiest type of return on the continuum), but you increase your risk and your return from being purely risk-free (the lowest type of return on the continuum). Thus, if you spread capital across the capital structure, one will end up with a rate of return roughly in the middle of the risk-continuum at a risk roughly in the middle of the risk-continuum. That is to say, moderate risk for moderate return. In simple terms,

[65] Strictly speaking, "diversifying" across a capital structure, isn't true "diversification", but is often colloquially confused as being the same concept.

allocating capital across the capital structure has the effect of averaging the return and risk across the capital structure.

However, if you are particularly mathematically inclined, you might realize that statistically speaking, taking a broad swath of the capital structure, is mathematically the same (or at least highly similar) as finding the "risk-return" median in the risk continuum, which should provide roughly the same "risk-return" proposition as the "mean". That is to say, it might seem like it would make sense simply to purchase some medium-grade, medium-yielding bonds rather than take the time to allocate capital across the entire capital structure.

While superficially, this math is accurate, it actually does not tell the whole picture in practicality. That is to say, simply selecting middle of the road assets in the risk-continuum (at the "median") will actually provide "risk-adjusted return" inferior to the "risk-adjusted return" from averaging together each component of the risk-continuum. The reason for this is that at the edges of the capital structure, the risk-adjusted return is superior. Said another way, at the far end of the safe side of the risk continuum, there is little to no risk of principal loss or loss of expected cash flows (although the return is at the "risk-free" or only mildly better than the "risk-free rate"). At the other side of the risky end of the continuum, the return (from common equity) is so high that it tends to pay back the full principal amount in return before any loss of principal is experienced and the cash flow tends to be so robust that the volatility in the expectation of future cash flows is tolerable.

As a result of the inverse relationship of risk-to-return, the middle of the continuum is actually the least safe area of the risk-continuum on a risk-adjusted basis, because it does not provide enough return to account for the risk of loss of principal and future expected cash flows. Additionally, because a lot of unusual and highly complex financial structuring tends to occur in the middle of the capital structure, the risk of principal loss tends to be higher than anticipated or reported. That is to say, high risk of loss tends to masquerade as medium risk-medium yielding.

Following this logic through to its natural conclusion, while investing in assets across the risk-continuum will give a better risk-adjusted return than purchasing the median risk-asset, it will provide an inferior risk-adjusted return to hollowing out the risk-continuum and simply investing in the safest and most risky levels of the risk-continuum (since by adjusting one's allocations between each side of the "barbell" one can effectively toggle the rate of return and rate of safety). This will be discussed more fully in the "barbell strategy" section below.

Interestingly, for most people this will seem initially counter-intuitive. That is to say, generally speaking in life, people tend to flock to the "average" or things in the "middle of the fairway" because there is perceived safety in the crowding. The idea of being in the "middle" seems safe. Ironically, this tends not to be the case (in finance and in life). One is typically better off on either side of the bell curve than in the middle.

Before we move on, it is important to mention that portfolios that allocate across the capital structure, are also typically diversified on the underlying productive asset level. That is to say, that allocating across the capital structure (or using the barbell structure), is usually more effective if there is diversification in the productive asset being relied upon for cashflow (such that exposure is not limited to the production of one single asset).

This should be fairly intuitive, as a matter of mathematics, since it would be somewhat perverse to lend to a productive asset to provide leverage to boost your own earnings, to which you are entitled to because you hold equity (you could get the same result likely by just owning more equity in such case). That is not to say, that doing so wouldn't adjust your risk-return profile, because it would (you would be entitled to a smaller return and have access to collateral, ahead of your other equity holders, if you were a senior secured lender for instance, which would adjust the risk-adjusted return if you just held equity). This just tends not to be done, because people usually select a type of exposure to an asset with which they feel comfortable and tend to invest entirely at that level. Additionally, investors tend not to give themselves leverage[66], since this would undermine the general purpose of leverage, which is to use other people's money to increase purchasing power to increase equity returns.[67]

---

[66] At least not knowingly, although sometimes investment in a debt fund and an equity fund will result in exposure to the same underlying asset twice if the manager is unscrupulous or the investor is not particularly diligent.

[67] By way of example, if I have a house and I am the sole equity holder in the house, it makes no mathematically sense to provide myself with debt on the house, because neither my returns nor property rights would change and my exposure to the asset would be the same. If I own 50% of equity and someone else owns 50% of equity and I provide senior secured debt to the house with the house as collateral, the end result would be that I increase my exposure to the house and create a property right in the house that exceeds the priority of my other equity holder (which might be desirable if I don't desire to just buy out the other equity holder). Generally, speaking though, I wouldn't benefit from the leverage provided (other than the property

3) Market Timing

The third strategy for increasing risk-adjusted return is the strategy of market timing. Market timing is fairly controversial, because most people believe it is not possible to do effectively. That is to say, most people are not good at timing the growth cycle of productive assets.

As we have already discussed, price is often mismatched with value. It is either over-priced or under-priced. If one makes a purchase during a time of under-pricing and sells during periods of over-pricing, one's returns will be better than if they purchase during times of over-pricing and sell during times of "under-pricing". Putting price aside for a minute and speaking about value, an investor will generally preform better, if they invest in an asset earlier in the growth cycle rather than later, because there is more potential for unrealized value in the beginning of the growth cycle than at the end of such cycle.

Unfortunately, as we have already discussed, people are mimetic, so people tend not to recognize value until

---

priority benefits) because the additional return I receive in increased equity returns is the result of my own contributed purchasing power (although the other equity holder would enjoy the benefit of the leverage). This is sometimes done by unscrupulous fund managers, who run both debt funds and equity funds simultaneously, because it can juice the return to the equity investors who do not provide the leverage (typically the manager themselves), typically at a favorable lending rate from a credit-risk perspective. From a security position, however, this will force a bankruptcy court to have to prioritize certain equity investors over others (that is to say the equity investors who also contributed debt will be entitled to underlying assets before the other equity holders), which is generally speaking a breach of the fiduciary duty of managers to treat all clients equitably (absent an express client consent waiver).

there is a track record or other people have already validated that value, so they tend to enter an investment late in the growth phase and just in time for the decay phase.

Of course, if an investor is aware of the mimetic process and uses it to their advantage one enjoys a significant increase in their return relative to their risk of loss. The danger is that the converse is also true, if one times the market incorrectly one reduces one's return relative to an increase in the risk of loss.[68]

In any case, generally speaking, like price, there is no real way to get around timing. That is to say, if you are going to make a purchase, you are going to make it sometime over the course of your life and therefore, even if you hate the idea of "market timing", there will be an element of time which cannot be avoided (since it is an essential aspect of Newtonian physics that cannot be avoided in the physical world). There are a number of strategies to deal with this fact.

The first is to ignore timing in its entirety. That is to say, to invest without any regard to timing. The end result of this is that sometimes one will invest late in the growth phase and sometimes one will invest early in the growth phase and over time that will average out to being somewhere in the middle of the growth phase, which generally speaking, is better than trying to time the market, timing it wrong, and always entering during the decay

---

[68] Interestingly, when people first become familiar with the financial markets, people tend to be attracted to timing the market. They then tend to get burned by it and then claim it isn't possible. A select few individuals continue to try until they figure out a system for timing the market and then they tend to get pretty rich, pretty quick (relative to others).

phase. This sounds fairly defeatist, because it is, but for most people who are really quite bad at market timing, this is better than the alternative. If all else fails, the law of averages work just fine.

The second strategy is to determine whether something is relatively under- or over-priced using some fundamental metric and to use that metric as a guide such that one tends to invest when things are under-priced. We are already familiar with this idea from Chapter 12, where we investigated using the difference between market-capitalization and nominal GDP to determine whether the U.S. economy was generally speaking relatively over-or under-priced relative to its income producing value.[69]

The third strategy uses "technical analysis", which is a financial way of saying using physics and generally involves using an understanding of Newtonian physics to determine whether a growth phase is beginning or ending. This primarily involves understanding that time is a vector. That is to say it is a force that pulls us all horizontally into the future. Price (which incorporates value to some degree) is also a vector which moves vertically (that is to say price can rise or fall). Calculating the combined force of these two vectors will create an angular vector (that is to say linear force exhibited at an angle of degree somewhere between the vertical and horizontal force in proportion to

[69] This tends to be a hallmark of valuing investing, despite the fact most value investors will vehemently deny timing plays any role. Value investors tend to view themselves as separate from market timers because they only time purchases and never sales, since in true value investing there never is a sale, but the fact remains, there is an element of timing that cannot be avoided and is often considered albeit within the context of determining whether something is over- or- under- priced.

the aggregated magnitude of the two forces), which one can use, within a range of probability, to approximate future prices over a designated time horizon. The simplest way to perform this calculation will be using linear regression or a trend line and by measuring acceleration. We will discuss this in more detail later in Chapter 18.

It is important to mention that a latent danger of market timing is the "transaction cost" associated with purchasing or selling assets. Said another way, there tends to be a certain amount of costs incurred when purchasing or selling an asset. When you sell a house for instance there are a series of inspections, legal fees and closing costs that must be performed. Similarly, when selling public stocks there is a bid-ask spread and a transaction cost associated with selling or purchasing a security (typically a brokerage fee for instance). When selling a private company there are inherent legal diligence and legal costs that must be paid for (as well as the structuring of the sale or purchase, sourcing capital, etc.). Transaction costs are important to consider, because it is conceivable if transaction costs are high enough, that they can erode the potential gain that would result from properly timing the growth cycle.

It is also important to reiterate that because humans tend to be mimetic, market timing tends to fly in the face of most people's natural emotional inclinations. The undisciplined tend to be particularly bad at it and it tends to take a toll emotionally on people even if they are successful at it (discipline and temperament are probably the two most important factors in doing it well).[70]

[70] Generally speaking, discipline and temperament are two of the most important aspects of being a good investor using any strategy.

4) Hedging / Insurance

The fourth strategy for increasing risk-adjusted returns is hedging. Hedging involves taking on a risk opposite of the risk to an asset you own, such that the gains to the "hedge" account for any proportional short-term loss suffered to your asset.

Hedging is extremely common, although many people do not realize it (it is often also government mandated). By way of real world example, insurance generally speaking is a hedge against a risk of loss. If you own a home and you have homeowners insurance, you pay a premium (typically monthly) to an insurance company, who accepts that premium in return for the obligation to pay you the market value of your home if it is destroyed (subject to various limitations listed in the policy which they will not cover; such as self-destruction for instance). Said another way, you and your insurance company have created a contract allocating the risk of loss of your asset. You have agreed to pay a fee to your insurance company for the benefit of having the insurance company bear the risk of something destructive happening to the value of the asset you own. This is referred to in financial speak as a "covered hedge". That is to say, the individual who owns the asset has hedged against the risk of loss of that asset.

Generally speaking, all insurance works this same way. Health insurance is a premium you pay to an insurance company who bears the risk of loss of you getting sick. Car insurance is a premium you pay to an insurance company who bears the risk of your car getting destroyed. Insurance can be placed on an asset of value, provided you can get someone to take the contracted risk of loss.

If you own an asset, purchasing insurance for such asset can be beneficial, because it protects against the risk of loss and if you do not pay more in premiums (aka the fee) than the value the asset produces or appreciates, then you enjoy return without the risk of loss (or said another way, if the premium cost to risk of loss calculation is done correctly one increases their "risk-adjusted return").

Interestingly, on a large scale (and because people on the whole are reasonable in their general conduct), insurance companies tend to enjoy profitability, because most individuals will never incur a risk of loss (or will incur such loss with such infrequency that the premiums will more than pay for the payout required when a claim of loss is made). That is to say on the whole, everyone tends not to fall deathly at the same time, yet everyone pays a premium to an insurance company, because no one wants to be saddled with the tremendous expense that comes with being deathly ill.[71]

In any case, the point here is that risk of loss can be allocated and shifted to others willing to take such risk by contract. Generally speaking, from the insurance company's perspective, the continuum of the trade is that it is most probable that nothing catastrophic will happen (and premiums will be enjoyed without having to pay out an excess of the premiums received in claims), and in the improbable event something catastrophic does happen on the whole the catastrophic event will not happen to everyone paying a premium. From the individual's perspective, if you happen to be one of the unlucky few to

[71] In the U.S. it is also government mandated so you have to individuals do not have a legal choice anyway, which creates government mandated demand.

whom a catastrophic event of loss occurs, someone else bears the financial risk of that catastrophic loss.

Said another way, one is willing to accept another's risk of loss, in exchange for a fee, if they believe that in the aggregate they will receive more in premium than they will pay out in claims. One is willing to pay a premium to offset the risk of loss, if one wishes to protect the value of their underlying assets. Said simply, insurance is an allocation of risk based on the probability of loss relative to the magnitude of loss.

In this way, insurance companies in some ways resemble banks[72], in that they take premiums (which while it is a fee paid to them, has a cost of capital associated with it, mainly the probability that they will need to pay the premiums received out in a claim and the magnitude of that potential claim) and they invest said premium, such that, provided a claim is not made immediately, the premium creates income from investment, which exceeds any potential claim to risk of loss. That is to say, they earn a spread based on the time value of money and the successfulness of their investment strategy, because they take money today in exchange for a potential obligation in the future, and in the interim earn a return (if done correctly in excess of any potential claim). In financial speak, when insurance companies invest premiums to earn a return to offset future obligations, this is referred to as "asset-liability" matching.

[72] Despite resembling banks, insurance companies tend to be less regulated by banks. This may change with time as government mandated demand will probably require some kind of price control and excessive risk taking may ultimately require a federal government bailout to systemically important financial institutions which might result in public opinion requiring greater oversight.

For the sake of completeness, it is important to note that insurance can also be purchased to insure against the risk of loss to assets that belong to someone else (in common parlance a "naked" hedge). To be clear, insurance against someone else's risk of loss is not a hedge per se, but rather a speculative bet that someone will endure loss. This is a form of a "derivative" transaction by which a party to a derivative transaction can be paid an insurance claim against someone else's loss in exchange for premiums. If the premiums paid are less than the payout resulting from an asset's loss, the bet is a winner. If more premiums are paid than paid out at the time of the asset's loss, it is a loser.[73]

In addition to insurance to hedge against risk of loss, there are a number of other contractual arrangements which can accomplish a hedge. In fact, almost any

---

[73] As a brief, but interesting aside, in the financial crisis AIG underwrote a great deal of insurance policies (or, more accurately, derivatives resembling insurance), which were serving as "naked hedges". That is to say, many financial institutions recognized that certain structured financial products sold as "assets" where inherently flawed and subject to fail (ironically many of the financial institutions that "recognized" this were the ones who created and sold the exotic financial products likely to fail). AIG for its part did not recognize the inherent risk in these products and took the premiums and used them. When these assets ultimately endured loss and the claims became due, AIG did not have the premiums (or invested income from such premiums) to pay the amount of claims owed, which would have pushed AIG into insolvency. Because AIG is systemically important (in that it is one of the largest insurers in the United States of America), the federal government realized allowing it to fail would cause ripple effects throughout the U.S. economy. This was one of the central reasons for the need for the "Troubled Asset Relief Program" (TARP), in 2009 and one of the reasons many of the financial institutions who assisted in causing the financial crisis, actually received a payout from the taxpayer (albeit through the conduit of AIG).

derivative product can be used as a hedge (that is to say any contract whose value is pegged to an underlying asset, can serve, and probably at its creation was intended to serve, as a hedge, including but not limited to options, swaps, futures, etc.). As an example, a power plant that uses electricity by burning natural gas might look at its financial situation and realize it can only produce electricity profitably if the price of the natural gas commodity it is burning is below a certain level (in common usage referred to as the "spark spread"). To prevent having to endure a negative spark spread, a power plant might, quite effectively, enter into a hedging transaction, by which the power plant agrees to have the option to buy natural gas at a set price (referred to as a "call option"). If the market price of natural gas goes above the call option, the call option will be "in the money". That is to say, despite the fact that the price of natural gas has made the spark spread unfavorable, the ability to continue to purchase the price of natural gas at a cost which keeps the spark spread profitable, will put the power plant in a positive financial position (despite the fact most of the market of natural gas plants who were not as foresighted will suffer). Once again, the fundamental calculation to determine the profitability of such hedge, will be a comparison of the premium paid for the right to purchase the natural gas at the price lower than the market price relative to the profit received from purchasing the natural gas at the price lower than market price. If this math is done correctly, it is a profitable hedge.[74]

---

[74] It should also be noted that options and derivatives generally can be used to speculate on price movements without taking the full risk of buying the underlying asset. Thus, in addition to use as a hedge, derivatives tend to be a robust and liquid market full of people

To be clear a hedge does not necessarily need to take the form of a derivative. Referring back to our example in the diversification section regarding inversely correlated assets, the purchase of a perfectly inversely correlated asset could serve as a hedge. That is to say, as the value of one asset increased the other would decrease and vice-versa. Generally speaking however, two perfectly inversely correlated assets will have the effect of canceling the majority of the other's returns and as such tends to be less useful than using a derivative, which gives the same exposure at less of a cost.

Similarly, referring back to our conversation on market timing, many market timers prefer to use derivatives to hedge (or to take a position on market timing) rather than to completely sell all of the assets in their portfolio. If done correctly, this could be beneficial, because it could potentially decrease costs of protecting one's portfolio (if the premiums are cheaper than the transaction costs of selling the portfolio), easier and more liquid (in that it typically takes less effort and time to enter into a contract than to sell an entire portfolio of assets), and is less risky from an opportunity cost perspective (derivatives are typically linked to a time horizon, if the event doesn't occur within the time period the hedge falls away albeit at the cost of the premium, if one sold their entire portfolio and the market event doesn't materialize, there will be an opportunity cost of the loss of the return that could have been had).

The danger to hedging is that premiums can be expensive (and can be miscalculated) and tend to be fairly speculative (that is to say they tend to depend on market

---

generally speculating on future events.

timing, at which people are rarely successful). However, as seen in the insurance example, hedging can provide significant peace of mind and significantly lower "risk-adjusted returns" (by significantly reducing the risk of loss) if done in a disciplined and properly calculated manner.

5) Indexing/Cost Reduction

The fifth strategy for increasing "risk-adjusted return" is known as "indexing", which was pioneered by the legendary investor (and founder of Vanguard®) Jack Bogle. Jack Bogle's book "The Little Book of Common Sense Investing" is one of the best books on investing ever written. To be clear, I have no association with Jack Bogle, other than to say that I have read his book and have generally admired his investing career.

My understanding of Jack Bogle's central thesis, is that while these strategies of diversification, hedging, and market timing exist, in the public markets people tend not to do these things very well. That is to say, by their nature people (including professionals in the industry) tend not to properly employ strategies that will increase "risk-adjusted return", but rather tend to decrease returns by ignoring latent risks (like transaction costs) and generally increase risk, rather than reduce it by doing things improperly. Further, the few people who are good at these strategies and put themselves in the marketplace to employ these strategies for other people, tend to charge a high fee for their work, because they know it is hard, they know there is demand for doing it right, and they know they are in short supply. As a result, the fees charged over time by these individuals tend to be high and these high fees tend to erode the gains that result from employing these strategies well, to the point that even if the manager increases risk-adjusted return (and to be clear they often don't because they to do it wrong), any benefit gained tends to be cancelled out by the high-cost of their services over time.

Understanding this fact, Jack Bogle's central thesis as I understand it, is to simply take overall market risk. That is to say, if you buy a fund or company that has as its underlying assets all of the U.S. marketplace (such that the investor has total market exposure), such fund can charge low to almost no fee (because there is no need to actively manage or continually rebalance the portfolio, so there is generally not terribly much to do), while delivering whatever return the market offers (which tends to be fairly safe, because, at least in the U.S. the value of the market, aka the whole economy, tends to increase with time as we have already discussed).

Thus, by eliminating the costs associated with "active" investing and enjoying the "passive" growth of the overall market, one can actually beat the returns provided by "active" managers because there is no cost erosion and active managers tend not to out-perform the market to any great extent in any case (if they out-perform the market at all). In modern times, this is referred to as "passive" v. "active" investing.

This strategy has the additional benefit of not being particularly difficult or emotionally draining. That is to say, it is both conceptually and practically easy. When you have money, you put it in a fund that gives you overall market exposure at low to no cost and you leave it alone forever (or until you need it for some life event).

Generally, speaking this strategy is often also combined with the "law of averaging" as we discussed earlier in "market timing", because the goal is to take market timing completely out of the equation. Thus, you pay little attention to whether the market is over- or under-priced and you invest in set intervals, with the knowledge that over time your overall cost basis will be "neutrally" or "fairly" priced (that is, neither over- or under- priced).

For most people, this strategy of "indexing" tends to be highly effective. It eliminates the mimetic cycle (by effectively ignoring it) and performance does tend to exceed active management (which people are generally not as good at as they think they are) over the long term.

The down-side to this strategy is that there is no real improvement in one's "risk-adjusted return", that is to say, the strategy is based on the principal that one's risk-adjusted return cannot really be manipulated (or at least is hard to improve) and as such one should just accept the return for the corresponding risk. You just take what the defense gives you.

To be fair, it is important to note, that while indexing may initially seem like tossing out all strategies to the wind, in favor of keeping costs low, indexing is actually a form of employing two strategies, we've already discussed (it just doesn't seem that way).

First, if you are playing close attention, you might realize that indexing is essentially diversification taken to an extreme. However, rather than diversify on the basis of correlation, you just buy a share of the entire economy. Doing this is the ultimate diversification, in that rather than have a large share in a few things, you have a small share in everything, and therefore have no exposure to the performance of individual assets, but rather share in the aggregate performance of society.

Second, indexing does not concern itself with where an investor chooses to invest in the "capital structure". That is to say, indexing does not occur across the capital structure typically, but rather indexing tends to occur across a class of assets. That is to say, there might be an index for the entirety of U.S. equity, an index for U.S. government bonds, an index for foreign government bonds, an index for investment grade debt, an index for high-yield (or junk) debt, etc. In fact, as people in the investment community have come to realize the value of "indexing" the demand for indexing has grown dramatically (which ironically has resulted in rather sophisticated financial instruments that seek to add back "active" management or "weighted-exposure to certain assets" into "indexed funds" or to add leverage in the form of various "leveraged exchange traded funds", which is the exact opposite of what an investor should be trying to do).

In the modern age, indexing is primarily done through the form of a mutual fund or an exchange-traded fund, both of which usually have an "R-squared" calculation which evidences how well the fund is tracking a benchmark (like the S&P index for instance).

6) Barbell Strategy

As can be seen, even if one wants to completely, insulate themselves from any real sort of decision making by indexing, one is still left with the question of the risk-continuum. That is to say, at what level of the capital structure does it make the most sense to invest.

Generally speaking, people have traditionally thought to buy an allocation of each level (usually leaving out the more exotic levels like "mezz-debt"), because in most people's view average risk across the continuum seems best. To be sure there is some truth to this since while mathematically averaging provides the same return as purchasing the median risk asset, it does provide a better "risk-adjusted return", because the assets on the far sides of the continuum are property rights (rather than contractual rights), which by their nature diminish the risk of loss (and thereby increase one's "risk-adjusted return").

However, as alluded to earlier, mathematically one can generate the same return of "averaging" across the risk continuum without having to accept the risk across the continuum by simply hallowing out the risk-continuum and purchasing assets which sit on either end of the risk continuum. Conceptually, you can think of this as a "barbell" (since there is weighting at either side and nothing in the middle of the allocation across the risk-continuum).

The reason one can generate the same return of averaging using the barbell structure, is because mathematically, one can allocate capital between the risk-free rate (or high-quality investment grade rate) and common equity in proportions which adjust the rate of return one will receive. By way of example, theoretically one could split capital between 50% risk-free (at a rate of return of say 3%) and 50% equity market (indexed say for an annualized rate of return of 15%), to arrive at an average annualized rate of return of 9%. This rate of return of 9% would be roughly equivalent to the return that could be expected by purchasing assets in the middle of the capital structure (i.e. a 9% return is roughly equivalent to the expected return for "high-yield" debt, which we know to be fairly dangerous and prone to loss). Similarly, this rate of return of 9% would be roughly equivalent to averaging all of the returns across the continuum. However, unlike buying assets in the middle of the capital structure or averaging all of the returns across the continuum, the risk of loss from the barbell strategy should be at all times quite low (that is to say, one would enjoy a much higher risk-adjusted return than one could expect to receive from a portfolio of high-yield debt or a portfolio of every asset in the capital structure).

The reason that the risk of loss is so low for the barbell strategy is that at the risk-free end of the continuum there is no risk of loss (albeit the return is also low[75]) and at the common equity end of the continuum there is a risk of total loss[76], but the return is so high that it is highly probably the investor will be compensated for that risk far before loss is endured.

As an example, on the risk-free side, if I have a portfolio of U.S. government debt, I can be sure that unless there's widespread political strife, I will receive my principal and my return.[77] Similarly, if I purchase senior

---

[75] Although the certainty of this return is high, because of senior secured debt's position in the capital structure, it is paid out first (that is to say it ranks first in priority of payment) and tends to get paid out even in a distressed scenario, unless the productive asset is a total loss.

[76] If the common equity investment is made in the form of a broad public market index fund which provides total equity market exposure to the public markets, the maximum risk of loss would more likely be approximately 50%, since historically market recessions typically result in a roughly 50% decline from the market high.

secured debt (that has for its collateral a real asset with no latent risks in the documentation), I can be sure that there will be no risk to my principal, because in the event of distress, I can go seize a real asset of compensatory value (although there would be some transaction costs and enforcement costs of foreclosing on such asset)[78]. On the total-risk side, at a 15% annualized rate of return, my expected return doubles my principal in roughly 5 years (which as we know tends to be only half the growth phase of the overall economy), which is more than enough to compensate me for total loss of my investment[79].

Additionally, such a strategy can be adjusted to target a designated return. As an example, if you need return higher than 9%, you allocate more capital to the equity side of the risk-continuum. If you need more safety, you allocate more capital to the risk-free side of the risk-continuum (at the expense of some additional return).

---

[77] This assumes of course that government debt is not negative. One would not invest into a negative yielding instrument from which they would receive no or negative return.

[78] One could also effectively purchase an index fund of high-quality debt to avoid having to foreclose and to give similar performance, without having to evaluate individual loans or maintain a loan book.

[79] Additionally, the loss I will suffer (again looking at the overall economy) tends to be less than the total growth achieved (that is to say the U.S. economy because of its structure, tends to grow with time, despite 3-year periods of decline, which tend to decline 50% on average from the total growth, that is to say every 10 years you give back half, then get 10 more years of 15% annualized growth from that new base. This example assumes, margin loans weren't used. Typically, during a 50% decline margin calls will be issued forcing the shares that serve as collateral to be sold and the profits used to collateralize the lender. At such point, the investor would lose all principal and underlying assets to the lender. Which for the equity investor would likely be a catastrophic event.

Thus, it is quite easy to see that by simply toggling between the highest risk and the lowest risk in the capital structure, one can achieve a desired return at decreased risk, because at each side of the continuum the extremity of the return relative to the risk is a fairly safe proxy for protecting one's principal investment (i.e. the risk at either side of the continuum is precisely inverse such that one side provides total return benefits and the other side provides total safety benefit and thereby allocating between the two provides additional safety depending on an individual investor's return needs, but in either case risk of principal loss is minimized). As you might expect, this gives you a superior "risk-adjusted return" than any of the other "allocation across capital structure" strategies because in either case the risk of principal loss is diminished to a greater extent than it would be anywhere in the middle of the risk-continuum.

The barbell strategy also has the additional benefit of avoiding any exotic financial and complex legal structures latent with hidden risks, because those tend to occur in the middle of the risk-continuum (where the tug of war is occurring in the Wild West of the contract world between the proper balance of risk and return). That is to say, you are much more likely to get what you paid for, in an honest forthright way, on either side of the risk continuum than you will in the middle (due in part to the fact on either side you have a property right in a real asset and not some pseudo-claim to property).

For proof of this mathematical concept please see the list of expected returns below:

Hypothetical Example of Expected Returns:

US Government debt (risk-free rate and duration risk): 2-3% depending on the duration

Investment grade debt: 3-6% depending on duration and rating

High yield debt: 5-9%

Mezzanine debt: 7-12%[80]

Preferred equity: 7-12%[81]

Common Equity: >15%

Average yield in portfolio of equal weight across the continuum[82] = ~6.25% - ~8.25%

Barbell return equal weight across barbell[83] = ~8.5% - ~9%

Real Returns over the last 10 years:

U.S. 10 year treasury (07/2009): ~3.481%[84]

Investment Grade Bond Fund (07/2009): ~6.25%[85]

High Yield Bond Fund: ~9.20%[86]

---

[80] This can be as high as 10-19% including equity incentives, but the class of asset will be ignored because it is not included in the typical investment portfolio.

[81] This can be as high as 10-15% including accrued returns and other kickers but the class of asset will be ignored because it is not included in the typical portfolio.

[82] (US Gov Debt + IG Debt + HY Debt + Common Equity)/4

[83] (US Gov Debt + Common Equity)/2

[84] https://www.cnbc.com/quotes/?symbol=US10Y

[85] https://fred.stlouisfed.org/series/HQMCB10YR

[86] Bank of America Merrill Lynch U.S. High Yield Master Ii Constrained

Common Equity Return of S&P 500 (annualized since 07/2009): ~23.15%

Average yield in portfolio of equal weight across the continuum = ~10.52%

Barbell return equal weight across barbell = ~13.32%

It is worth noting above that the barbell strategy's nominal return actual exceeds that of averaging across the capital structure. When considered from a "risk-adjusted" perspective, the return of the barbell structure is further superior, because the risk of loss of principal is significantly reduced, relative to a portfolio that contains exposure to investment grade (specifically below A rated investment grade bonds) and high yield bonds.

Interestingly the barbell strategy is one of the oldest strategies in the books (although it was not characterized as a barbell, but rather a "bond-equity" strategy in days past). It is so old in fact that you may not be aware of it unless you are over the age of 65. It is the original model and so old as to have been forgotten by many in the modern age.

That is to say, the old adage in investing (before there was complex financial structuring and engineering), was to allocate some capital to government or senior secured bonds and some capital to equity. When you were young you were told to purchase more equity (because return is more important than risk at a young age since you can wait out market fluctuations and typically have less money accumulated at this stage in one's life) and when

---

Index (ICE BAML US HY/HY Const B) ten year annual total returns. https://fundresearch.fidelity.com/mutual-funds/summary/316062108

you are old you increase your allocation of bonds (because you want the steady, albeit low, income and not to lose the money you saved over the course of your life).

Despite being the old (and perhaps slightly boring) strategy, the math supports that it is in fact the best strategy from a "risk-adjusted return" perspective, whether you are an individual or an institution.

In fact, for institutional investors, I suspect performance would be much improved by having only two main allocations of capital. One main allocation to government bonds (mainly U.S. treasuries) and AAA/AA (high-grade investment grade debt) all of which is senior secured with collateral that are real assets, and one main allocation to equity (whether that be private equity, public equity or real estate assets). The benefit of doing so, is that the spread between the high quality debt and equity would exceed returns and eliminate risk of loss (for the most part) rather than continually suffering loss at the hands of highly complex financial structures or BBB debt that operates at the end of investment grade (neither of which are providing proper compensation for latent risk taken in any case).[87]

---

[87] Additionally, because large financial institutions (pension funds, insurance companies, etc.) are not permitted by law/regulation to hold junk debt, the flight from junk debt that results when large swaths of BBB-investment grade debt gets downgraded to junk status, tends to cause a spiral of asset value decay. That is to say, the aggregation of pension funds, insurance companies and financial institutions tend to serve as funnels which aggregate the majority of the world's wealth into various investments. When these institutions begin selling at the same time (because they are mandated by law/regulation to do so or otherwise), there are insufficient buyers to counter-act the force of selling or said another way, to allow all of the sellers to find a buyer to which to sell. In such an environment, market "liquidity" dries up and tends to exacerbate selling and panic.

In such situations a crisis typically ensues (which often requires government intervention to curtail).

Chapter 15: Investing Strategies

Now that we properly understand some portfolio strategies for improving "risk-adjusted return" and curtailing risk, it is important to understand that there are numerous strategies individuals use to "invest" on an "asset-by-asset" level (or said another way, to select assets for investment).

There are three main types of "investing": "value investing", "growth investing" and "distressed investing".

1) Value Investing

The oldest and probably the most famous form of investing is "value investing". "Value investing" is the process by which one contributes capital (in the form of a purchase price) to acquire a productive asset (either in whole or in part), which one believes with time will produce "value" (i.e. "profit" or "earnings") sufficient to compensate and exceed the purchase price paid over time (with "profit" or "earnings" either paid out as income to such investor as a "dividend", or retained on the enterprises balance sheet such that the value of the enterprise increases as reflected in price appreciation).

To unpack this a bit, let's take this in stages. First, to be "value investing" the asset acquired must be "productive". That is to say, it must have the ability to produce earnings. If the asset acquired cannot produce earnings then you are not value investing. As an example, purchasing commodities is not value investing. A commodity can be bought or sold at a price which fluctuates based on relative supply and demand. A commodity can be bought or sold to be used for production, but a commodity itself cannot produce. Therefore, one cannot be a "value investor" if they primarily purchase commodities.

Second, assuming one has purchased a "productive asset", a productive assets "value" (as we have already discussed) will be determined by its productive ability. That is to say, the earnings or net profit it produces from its production. Depending on management's short-term and long-term plans for productivity, earnings can be dealt with in two main ways. One, it can be distributed out to the equity holders in proportion with their share of ownership (termed a "dividend") or it can be retained on the balance sheet (as "retained earnings"). Retained earnings accumulate on the balance sheet as shareholder equity, since practically what has happened is residual earnings that have trickled through the capital structure and technically belong to the equity holders have been left in the business for business use to increase the value of that business. As a concrete example, a business might retain earnings, so they have cash available to increase the production of their manufacturing plant (i.e. make a capital expenditure) thereby increasing productivity of their productive asset. Said another way, retained earnings are earnings reinvested in the productive asset by the equity holders to increase the value of the enterprise. Increased value retained by a productive asset tends to increase the value of an enterprise over time (and is typically reflected overtime in the purchase price, that is to say, the market price to purchase an asset tends to increase or "appreciate" as value increases).

In value investing, prior to purchasing a productive asset, a determination is made as to whether the productive value of the business over a time period will be sufficient to compensate one for the purchase price paid (the purchase price typically being higher than the value of the enterprise on day one and expressed as the Price-to-Earnings multiple as previously discussed). That is to say, for value investing, the goal is to acquire a productive asset that has value that will provide a return over time in excess of the principal investment.

To do this effectively, one will tend to want to make purchases when assets are "cheaply" valued (or "under-valued"). That is to say, the purchase price paid will be one of the most important factors in determining the rate of return (the others being the earnings produced and the time horizon for the investment). As such, value investors will usually use metrics to determine if a "price-to-earnings" multiple is warranted based on the certainty of future cash flows and the value of such cash flows in present value terms over an investing time horizon (typically using a NPV or discounted cash flow). As you might expect, the longer the time horizon the more likely one is to receive earnings in excess of one's purchase price (provided the expected earnings continue to materialize). As a result, to be done successfully value investing is a long-time horizon prospect. That is to say, you get rich slow, but you get very rich consistently overtime. The longer the productive asset produces expected future cash flow, the better one does.

To be clear, for most value investors the strategy is buy cheap and hold forever. There is no selling in the time horizon (because as long as the asset produces value past the point one receives their principal allocation back, one receives value forever at the relatively low cost of maintaining one's interest in the enterprise). It is a buy and hold and collect income/retained earnings strategy.

By way of example, as a "bond investor", I might employ a strategy of "value investing", by which I purchase a bond for the rate of return set forth at the time of issuance. For instance, if a bond is issued with a 5% interest rate and trades at a price 80% of par (that is to say, at a 20% discount of price), if I purchase that bond and hold to maturity, I will receive the benefit of 5% plus an additional yield for purchasing at a discount, or in this example a yield of 6.25% (because I bought cheaply my rate of return increased). My return continues until the productivity of my asset matures fully (that is to say, all of its value is used up and it goes extinct or dies).

Unlike a bond which has a set maturity stated at the time of issuance, for a value investor who is an "equity investor", the time horizon is often forever (although most enterprises tend to have a life span of somewhere between 10 and 100 years depending on how large and successful a productive asset or enterprise is) or as long as the productive asset produces cash flow.[88]

You will notice that in both instances, selling at an increased price did not play into the equation. If someone is purchasing an asset with the intention of selling it in the future, they are not investing, they are "trading" (even if done over an extremely long time horizon).

Additionally, if evaluating underlying value does not play into (really dominate) the determination to purchase (and the price of purchase), one is not value

---

[88] Although otherwise the calculations for determining the IRR for such equity investment is analogous to a bond's yield (and a productive life of an investment can be assumed to determine a yield-to-maturity).

investing. Just looking at "price" is not investing, it is trading.

Many people falsely think they are value investing because they purchase an asset with the expectation that the price will increase with time and they will sell at that time (usually far in the future) and pocket the appreciation in price. To be clear, this is not value investing. While appreciation in purchase price is a potential way, underlying value in an enterprise can be expressed (mainly as retained earnings), purchasing at a price expecting appreciation in price is not investing it is trading.

As you might expect because the time horizon for value investing tends to be a long-time period, value investors tend to seek out investments that will produce stable cashflow over a long period of time and are typically attracted to mature enterprises with proven cashflow that is consistent (that is to say not-volatile).

Additionally, with value investing (unlike some other forms of investing) not losing is far more important than winning. That is to say, it is more important that the entire portfolio of assets the value investor owns grows steadily with time, without any loss of principal, than it is important that a single asset in the portfolio outperforms and produces tremendous earnings growth/growth in value. Value investing is the turtle method, slow and steady wins the race.

Additionally, because the risk of loss is low, the time horizon is long and the rate of return is steady, value investors tend to greatly enjoy the benefit of compounding. That is to say, value investors tend to have reinvestment of value received (i.e. dividends or retained earnings) as a primary strategy for increasing value. Mathematically, the more value they reinvest, the more their value increases and the greater their value becomes. This is just like our hen example. If hens are a super stable line of business and return stable value over time, I can let my hens grow and multiply until I have a lot of valuable hens. The benefit of this mathematically, of course, is that one enjoys exponential rather than linear growth.

Interestingly, and perhaps somewhat arrogantly, most value investors believe that value investing is the only way to invest (or the only effective way to invest). This is not the case, but they may be right that overtime, generally speaking, it is the safest and most reliable way to invest. It certainly has a great track record of success.

I would also just caution that as a general rule, if someone tells you they are a value investor, but then never discuss any kind of underlying value or tell you about selling within a time frame, you can be pretty assured they are not a value investor (and generally are probably not to be trusted with your capital).

To be clear, value investing can be performed in either the public or private markets. That is to say you could successfully value invest by buying sandwich shops just as effectively as you could buying public stock corporations. The strategy is largely the same.[89]

---

[89] Although the ability to control net cash flow tends to vary significantly based on the size of an enterprise and whether an enterprise is public or private. In an enterprise you can purchase in full (whether public or private), it will be easier to control the net cashflow and distribute large dividends (or perhaps all of the profit) to oneself for further investment. Generally speaking, private enterprises tend to have smaller market capitalization than public

It can also be performed at any level of the risk-continuum although because the strategy is based on capital safety it makes more sense to do it at the riskiest end of the continuum (i.e. common equity), because that will generate the best returns (since the strategy itself decreases risk generally, the best return will be received by going to the riskiest side of the continuum). Additionally, (and as already discussed with the barbell strategy) attempting to value invest in the middle of the risk continuum will be counter-productive because you will have to endure periods of loss of expected cashflow and principal loss which will erode the benefits of compounding. One could effectively, "value invest" on the risk-free side of the risk-continuum, these returns will just be inferior to "value investing" on the riskiest side of the continuum (unless the risk-free rate is in the part of its long-term cycle where it is abnormally high, i.e. as it was in the 1980s).

Additionally, because value investing, properly conducted, occurs over such a long-time horizon with such stable cash flow, it is generally perfectly acceptable to use some form of leverage to increase purchasing power initially (since the sooner a purchase is made, the sooner you can enjoy the benefits of compounding). The danger of course is to use only an amount of leverage that keeps the asymmetry of risk in your favor. That is to say, if you bet the entire farm as part of your collateral, decay events

---

companies and are therefore easier to purchase in full. Additionally, public companies tend to have more robust cashflow restrictions and other stakeholders seeking access to such cashflow (or at least seeking to make decisions with regard to such cashflow). Being able to control net cashflow is important to value investing, because the value investor is highly incentivized to extract all free cashflow available for reinvestment (to fully realize the benefits of compounding).

in your productive assets will have the effect of significantly eroding the benefit of compounding value that is the hallmark of value investing. Said another way, going bankrupt because you overleveraged would defeat the whole purpose of value investing, because it destroys the ability to compound with time (by effectively destroying value periodically in accordance with the growth cycle of your productive assets). However, low to moderate leverage in value investing is common.

It is also important to note that once a portfolio of "value investments" has reached a certain size, it will tend to perform in accordance with the overall market (that is to say it will perform generally the same as indexing in rate of return terms).[90]

Before we finish, I would also just mention that because successful value investing is based on understanding the difference between price and value, value investing tends to have a component of market timing. That is not to say value investors are "market timers" (in fact most will vehemently deny market timing plays any role), but as you might expect if the entire market is under-valued relative to price it will be easier to find productive assets to purchase at an attractive price, as opposed to trying to find an attractively priced asset in a largely over-valued market (although it is certainly still possible).

In this way, value investors tend to time the market with their purchases. The glaring difference between a value investor and a market timer of course is that a value

---

[90] Although this is a good problem to have, as the portfolio will typically be of extraordinary value by the time this occurs.

investor never sells (or attempts to sell) during a market top (or what they believe to be a market top), so they avoid the mimetic process of selling at the wrong time (or becoming excessively emotional generally over market fluctuations), but they receive the benefit of making purchases at times when the market is under-valued, which tends to further boost risk-adjusted return relative to other strategies (superior to say purely averaging for instance).[91]

2) Growth Investing

The second type of investing in my view is "growth investing". Growth investing is more or less the inverse of "value investing". That is to say, in "value investing" one invests for the benefit of cashflow that is believed to be secure and consistent. In "growth investing" one invests for the benefit of cashflow that does not yet exist (and is therefore inherently speculative), but if it does materialize will exceed the cost of the initial investment. Said another way, "growth investing" is founded on investing early in the growth phase of a productive asset, before productivity has had an opportunity to ramp up and therefore before the purchase price reflects the value of the future cashflows of the mature productive asset. The most common form of this type of investing is "venture capital" or "start-up investing".

"Venture capital" is a process by which an investor allocates capital to a group or pool of "early-stage" enterprises or "pre-growth" phase enterprises. Because the enterprises are early in their life-cycles they are unlikely to

---

[91] Value investors tend to follow the market capitalization to GDP ratio, we discussed earlier, pretty religiously to get a general sense of the prospects of being able to make attractive purchases.

have any significant cashflow or said another way real financial value as an investment. As a result, the investor is able to command a large interest in the enterprise and a significant amount of control in the asset without allocating a great deal of capital compared to what the value of the enterprise would be at maturity (i.e. if expected cashflow materializes). Said another way, because the enterprise hasn't proven its value yet, its purchase price is discounted for the fact, its value might never materialize. Because growth in all productive assets tends to follow an exponential growth model because of the nature of compounding. If growth does materialize, the venture capitalist can expect to receive an extremely high return on their investment (that is to say it is not uncommon for a venture capital investment worth $100,000 ten years later to be worth $100 million or a 1,000 fold increase in value). The danger of course is that this style of investment is inherently speculative and there is no real way of knowing what early-stage enterprises will succeed and which will fail.

Venture capitalist investor's deal with this primarily by exposing themselves to a fairly large pool of assets. Because the investor has no real idea which asset in the pool is most likely to succeed (and which are likely to fail), the investor "diversifies" this risk by purchasing a pool of assets (like our diversification strategy above, but with no real focus on correlation of assets) with the expectation that in a large pool of assets as a matter of probability at least one is likely to succeed, and that success (if the growth rate is calculated appropriately) will exceed the value of the investment allocated to the entire pool. As we know, the growth phase of the average enterprise is generally 10 years, so typically venture capitalist investors have a ten-year time horizon after which they decide if an investment is worth keeping.

As you can see more clearly now, venture capitalism is more or less positioned on the opposite side of the continuum of investing. It is the inverse of the value investing strategy. In value investing every asset is expected to produce a consistent slow and steady return. In venture capital investing, one asset is expected to produce explosive cashflow growth that far exceeds the value not only of the purchase price of that productive asset, but the purchase price of all of the other assets in the venture capitalist's portfolio.

At its most extreme, venture capital takes the form of a single start-up. That is to say, if you are an entrepreneur with an idea, you are taking a completely undiversified risk, that the value of your enterprise (or idea) at maturity is worth the time, money and effort invested into creating that enterprise. Because you are essentially creating productivity out of thin air (that is to say the value of future cashflows of an enterprise is most certainly greater than an idea in one's head that produces no cashflow), the potential benefit of being a successful entrepreneur is on par with the payout of winning the lottery. That is to say, you can go from poor to rich in no time at all (typically around 10-20 years though). On the downside, the probability of failure is high (1 in 10 business fail after 10 years).

For the venture capitalist there are two important factors for success: 1) the magnitude of cashflows of a successful asset and 2) the number of assets in the portfolio that ultimately become successful. First, the greater the increase in value relative to the purchase price of the successful asset, the better the total portfolio return. Second, the more assets in the portfolio that succeed the greater the total portfolio return (because there are less laggards and more gains). As a result, to skew the probabilities in their favor, venture capitalists typically evaluate an investment based on a number of metrics or factors (usually non-cash metrics which they believe to increase the probability of a successful enterprise).

The first factor venture capitalists tend to use to evaluate an investment tends to be the size of the market and the potential of the enterprise to capture that market. Venture capitalists tend to focus on a market they believe to be "underserved" or new, innovative and untapped. The logic for this is that even the perfect productive asset will not succeed in growing beyond the size of its market. Think of the cells in my dish in the lab. No matter how great my cells are and how fast they grow, if the dish is small and the food supply is small, sooner or later they will run out of room and start dying. The same is true for an enterprise. It is difficult to grow beyond the number of consumers and even harder when there are already competitors selling to those consumers. Generally speaking, the larger the market and the less competitors that exist in the market, the better the prospects of future growth for a venture capitalist are.

The second factor, is typically how good the venture capitalist believes the idea to be. Said another way, how big a problem is the productive asset solving. As an example, if there is a robust supply of cows and I sell hens, I can probably expect that I won't sell that many hens because people have beef and beef tastes better. Conversely, if it is impossible to raise cows in my area and

I have the only chicken farm. I can now solve the problem of hunger, which can demand a high price and make me quite rich. Of course, this is inherently speculative (and many a venture capitalist has wrongly thrown away an idea which ultimately became a billion-dollar enterprise).

The third factor, is scaling. Said another way, how fast and at what expense can the productive asset grow. If I have a chicken farm and it takes me 20 years to raise the chickens necessary to meet the demand, even though there is tremendous demand, my supply of chickens cannot meet the supply fast enough for a venture capitalist to see rapid growth in their investment. Additionally, I will need continual capital improvements to my farm to increase my supply of chickens (because they need space to live) which will increase my costs as I scale and will erode profit as I grow. Conversely, if I start an internet company and the only additional cost I have from serving one person to serving 10 million is server space sold at $100 a month (regardless of size), then I can expect that profitably will grow quite rapidly, because scaling in revenue growth will far outpace additional costs undertaken to sustain that growth. Scaling is an extremely important factor to venture capitalists and one of the key reasons most venture capital in the modern day is focused on internet or technology firms. Internet and technology firms have extremely low scaling costs and they scale extremely rapidly by nature. As a result, one can become very rich very fast, with comparatively little effort as compared to an industrial company or more traditional enterprise, which relies on fixed assets (i.e. property, plants and equipment).

The fourth factor is management and talent. Rightly or wrongly, venture capitalists tend to favor giving money to individuals who already have a proven track record of success. That is to say, a successful entrepreneur is more likely to receive capital than a new or unsuccessful entrepreneur. This is generally founded in the belief that there is some innate talent or gift the management team has that others don't possess, that will result in success. This also tends to be inherently speculative, although I will admit that experience and knowing what to do is often of significant value to a new enterprise.

What you might notice from these factors is that none of them are "financial" in nature. That is to say, cashflow is typically not even considered as a factor (because it doesn't yet exist), even though potential future cashflow is the ultimate determinant of whether an investment is successful. Rather one must rely on "soft" data to determine projections for potential future cashflow and whether such cashflow will ultimately materialize.

Interestingly, because many of the most successful companies today are technology companies and such companies in their youth were valued based on these softer factors like "user growth", "user engagement", "time spent on the website", etc. These factors have leaked into their valuation when these companies reach maturity, even when listed on public stock exchanges. As such, the price to earnings multiples of technology companies tend to be unmoored from traditional multiple metrics (that is to say they tend to exceed the multiple that would seem reasonable to a value investor), as investors look to soft data to show that there is still room in the growth cycle for additional growth.

It is for this reason that many value investors "missed" or intentionally avoided technology companies despite their tremendous success (because the value investor's cashflow and financial metrics are not designed to account for these "growth" companies). It is also why technology stocks tend to be inherently speculative and subject to tremendous price to value mis-matches (as well as general price volatility).

Additionally, because investors tend to rely on the "soft data" to determine enterprise prices in technology, the technology firms have learned to engage in a fair bit of financial engineering.[92] That is to say, because they know that they will get a lofty valuation (or market capitalization) based on the soft data alone, they will often arrange their income statements such that their costs exceed their income. In a traditional enterprise this would be detrimental, because without reporting underlying value there would be no share price growth, but in a technology firm soft data is enough to induce share price growth. Reporting a loss (rather than a profit) has a number of benefits, including but not limited to the tax benefits of reporting a loss and the benefit of being able to spend any residual revenue on costs to produce additional rapid growth. It also tends to result in a general disregard generally for common shareholders by management (who tend to retain more wealth than they otherwise should).[93]

---

[92] Whereas making false statements about future cashflow projections would likely fall under price "manipulation" punishable by law, false statements about soft data like "user engagement" are more akin to "puffery" and less likely to land a corporate insider in trouble with a financial regulator, despite the fact for these types of enterprises, broad proclamations regarding soft data is likely to affect share prices.

[93] Since management pay is an accounting "cost" and founders of organizations tend to remain in management positions, the incentive to insiders to report a gain to receive share value is minimized, because they receive appreciative share value anyway as a result of

3) Distressed Investing

The final investment strategy we will discuss is "distressed investing". As the name suggests, distressed investing is a strategy by which an investor contributes capital to a productive asset that has because of some external or internal event suffered a loss event that has caused the price of such productive asset to become attractive relative to the residual value in that productive asset.

Distressed investing can take a few different forms, but generally speaking all distressed investing is based upon the fact that after a loss event (if the enterprise does not fail), price will tend to fall. If price falls low enough, it is possible that the remaining underlying value in the productive asset (after accounting for the loss from the loss event) is sufficient to result in a new increase in value to the investor. Said another way, if price falls too much or overreacts to a loss event, the price could be "cheap" enough that it is worth purchasing the asset in order to capture the value of future cash flows.

The danger of course to this strategy is if there is a systemic problem with the productive asset that will cause it to fail fully. Generally speaking, distressed investing is considered a fairly risky strategy (depending on the nature of the underlying assets purchased). However, when done correctly this strategy can be quite lucrative.

---

the soft data and receive income from salary. This significantly disincentives dividend distribution to common shareholders (and incentivizes "reinvestment" in the business for additional soft data growth, which in turn increases share prices until the growth can no longer be maintained by additional investment).

As an example, let's consider a senior secured bond secured against real tangible collateral. As we know from our discussion of the risk-continuum, we know that the risk of principal loss is typically fairly low, because the collateral should have adequate value to fully compensate the bondholder for the principal loss. Let's say hypothetically that a senior secured bond has suffered a loss event, that is to say the bond's issuer has defaulted on payments. The default will likely cause the market price of the bond to decrease (assuming there is a liquid market for the bond), that is to say, it will become available for purchase for below its initial issuing price or "par" value. Typically, the price of a bond relative to its par value will fluctuate along with the certainty of the expected future cashflow from that bond (or said in the opposite way the risk that those cashflows won't materialize). Also, typically a defaulted bond will receive a market price right around its recovery value. As an example, if a bond defaults it might trade at a 50% discount, if bondholders believe they will only receive 50% of the principal amount back in a bankruptcy proceeding. However, if an investor thinks that this bond is likely to perform (that is to say they believe the underlying productive asset will perform and the debt will be repaid and that the default is due to some temporary transitory factor), such investor would be incentivized to purchase this bond at the 50% discount being offered in the market. Purchasing the bond at a discount has the effect of increasing the "yield" one receives on the bond.[94] The danger of this strategy of

---

[94] As we have already discussed a bond has a notational face amount (known as the "par value") and an interest rate associated with such bond at issuance based on the face value (the "coupon rate"). If one pays a purchase price below the face value to acquire the right to the

course is that I may not receive the benefit of this discount or increased "yield", if the bond defaults and I don't receive the benefit of any future cashflows from my purchase. Generally speaking, however (in the case of senior secured bonds held against tangible collateral), I can be fairly confident that I will get the value out of my bond in bankruptcy (although I may run into liquidity issues, i.e. I may not be able to sell my bond because there may not be sufficient buyers or any buyers interested). There are, however, some inherent difficulties with having to get value out of collateral in bankruptcy, mainly that it takes time and expense to enforce on collateral and once received collateral tends to be illiquid and costly to maintain (for instance if I am a bondholder and my collateral is 1/1000th interest in an airport in Africa, it will likely be hard for me to realize this value by selling it or enjoying the benefit of it).[95]

As you might expect, distressed bond investing can be quite lucrative (if done correctly), but tends to require a certain level of financial expertise and therefore its benefit is typically only enjoyed by financial professionals.

---

interest rate being paid on the face amount of the bond, the "actual interest" rate received will be in excess of the coupon rate because the investor did not have to pay the face amount to acquire the interest being paid on the face amount. In real numbers, if a bond has a coupon rate of 10% on a face value of $1000, the "fixed income" the bond produces on the bond is $100. If I can acquire the bond for $500, the "yield" or the interest received on my money is equal to 20%.

[95] As we will see in the next chapter, purchasing a distressed asset for the purpose of realizing underlying collateral value is more akin to "trading" and wouldn't be considered as a strategy in this case, although it would mitigate some of the risk of being a distressed investor.

To be sure, distressed debt investing is not the only way to be a "distressed investor". One could buy real estate in a depressed area on the basis that rental income from the property will provide an attractive rate of return. One could purchase distressed equities on the same basis (although this tends to be fairly dangerous because you would be investing into the riskiest part of the capital structure, which entitles the equity holder to only residual profit and no principal protection, in an asset that has already shown itself to be struggling to meet its financial obligations).

Before moving on to the next chapter, it is important to note that all of the investing strategies discussed above require the ability to evaluate the underlying "fundamentals" of an investment to determine risk of loss to principal, the certainty of future cashflow and the value of that cashflow relative to the purchase price the market demands. As you can also readily see, all "investing" has at its core a basis in seeking to profit from a mis-match in the purchase price of an asset (whether because of a long-term investment horizon, timing of an investment in its lifecycle or temporary distress events) relative to the expected future cashflow that can be reasonably expected to be received from the production of the asset. While this future cash flow, when realized can be distributed to an investor in the form of income (as a dividend) or in the form of retained earnings (which increases the value of the enterprise and causes price appreciation), all investing is concerned with more than solely price appreciation. That is to say, investors, regardless of type, are concerned with realizing underlying value in a productive asset (which while it may be expressed in an increased price, is based on a fundamental increase in value). If you purchase an asset at a price with the sole expectation of price appreciation overtime, you are not investing, you are "trading".

Chapter 16: Trading on Fundamentals

Before we begin our discussion of trading, it is important to make the distinction between trading and investing clear.

As a starting point, the IRS generally defines income from investing as income which is earned over the course of more than one year. If income is earned on a productive asset (regardless of how this is accomplished) in one year or less, it is considered income from trading activity or "ordinary income" and is taxed as such. Based on this IRS definition, you might be misled into believing any capital allocation to an asset which you hold for more than a year is an "investment" and anything held for less than a year is a "trade". This is incorrect (yet many people believe this and organize their portfolio in this way).

The distinction between trading and investing is that investing (as we have already discussed) is concerned with paying a purchase price for underlying value that will be realized over time (as either income or retained earnings) and trading is concerned with paying a purchase price lower than one believes that purchase price will be in the future.

Conceptually and practically, this is a subtle yet important distinction. That is to say, the time horizon of a trade does not affect the fact that it is still a trade. If I purchase something today, with the expectation supply and demand forces are such that 20 years from now the purchase price will be higher and I will be able to sell at a profit (pocketing the spread in the price change), even though the time horizon is 20 years (and the IRS would classify this as income from investing), it is in fact a trade (albeit a long one). Conversely, if I purchased an asset today with the expectation that its future cashflows will exceed my purchase overtime, which will be expressed in an increased purchase price because of the retained earnings I expect, and 10 years later that asset's price in my portfolio has increased as a result, I am investing.

This is not to say, you cannot be successful at both trading and investing, you can. They are just different strategies which are not to be conflated.[96]

Maintaining the distinction between trading and investing is important because, generally speaking, trading is a riskier (or less certain) strategy than investing. It also tends to incentivize shorter term capital allocations. That is to say, in trading, the longer the duration the more "duration" risk a trade has.

Stepping back for a moment to take a closer look at investing. You will remember from the prior chapter that in the context of "value investing", a longer time horizon is a hallmark of being successful. That is to say, because we are relying on consistent cashflow, the more time we allow to transpire the more cashflow we can expect to collect. The more money we collect the better our investment, because it increases the spread of our profit relative to our purchase price. For investing, a longer-time horizon is a net benefit.

---

[96] To be fair to the IRS, the arbitrary distinction drawn between "investment" activities occurring within a year or over a year, serves to encourage long-term capital allocations to assets in the U.S. economy because it provides a tax benefit to allocating capital for longer than one year.

For trading, this paradigm is reversed, because we are not looking to capture any true value rather we are looking to capture price appreciation (which could occur for any host of reasons none of which are necessarily rational and most of which, even if rational, are inherently speculative). The longer we hold the trade, the more risk we have that some speculative and unforeseen force comes along and destroys the price, the more exposure we have to any costs of maintaining the asset we are trading (if there are any associated costs) and the more exposure we have to the "opportunity cost" of not purchasing some other asset that enjoys greater price appreciation. Mathematically, the longer a trade is held, the more time degrades the rate of return (since the gain made in the trade will be spread along a longer time period on an "annualized return basis"). Thus, this "time decay" works exponentially against a trader, unlike in investing where the passage of time leads to additional compounded value being received (and thus time works exponentially for the investor). This element of time is the essential characteristic distinguishing investing from trading.

As an example, let's say hypothetically we are interested in undeveloped land (known in colloquial industrial speak as a "greenfield") as an "investment". We look at the land and we realize that it would be a good place for a windfarm, because there is a consistent cross-breeze that blows over a mountain and out toward an ocean. We further believe that the difference in high and low pressure formations, which tend to form on either side of the mountain near the coast, results in a nice temperate plain that would generate a great deal of electricity if it had a windmill sitting atop it. Now let's say we do the math and we realize that if we purchase the land for $1 million and it takes another $9 million to build a windfarm, the windfarm will produce $2 million in revenue at an operating cost of $1 million or $1million in net cash flow annually. Additional research shows that the average life of a windfarm is approximately 20 to 25 years. Calculating in this average life we conclude that we should invest in this land and construct a windfarm, because after 20 years (the minimum expected life of our windfarm), we will have received $20 million for our investment of $10 million dollars today (at an annualized cash on cash rate of return of approximately 5%[97]). Additionally, if our windfarm lasts 25 years, we can expect to enjoy having received $25 million for our investment of $10 million dollars today over that 25 year period (at an annualized cash on cash return of approximately 10%). As you can see because the amount of cash we receive as return from our cash investment increases with time, we will be rooting for a long-lifespan for our investment.

Conversely, let's say we see the same greenfield as before. We look at the land and we draw the same conclusion that it would be an ideal place for a windfarm because of the terrain, weather pressure systems, and the nice flat plain. Now let's say we evaluate the price of the land and we realize the land is worth only $1 million today, because no one realizes it is a good place for a windfarm and everyone has generally discounted the land as being a bad place for farming, so it is lying vacant. Now let's say, based on this belief, we purchase the land for $1 million

[97] From an IRR or NPV perspective, the rate of return would be lower depending on the cost of capital from which we sourced the capital for the initial investment and the discount factor applicable to determine the time value of money, but cash on cash works fine for our example here.

dollars, because we do some research and we realize a parcel of land that ideal for wind farming should really be priced at $3 million dollars because the supply of land of this nature is relatively low (that is to say it is hard to find a flat parcel of land wedged between two consistent pressure systems that generate consistent air flow to spin the wind turbines). Once, we purchase the land we immediately begin looking for a windfarm developer who would be interested in buying the land. When we do, we sell it as soon as we find a buyer willing to pay the $3 million we expect to receive and pocket the spread as profit. That is to say, if we succeed in selling for $3 million and we purchased for $1 million, we enjoy the benefit of $2 million in trading profit.[98]

As you might expect, the longer we hold the position the worse our return becomes. That is to say, if we buy the land and sell it in one year our annualized cash on cash return is 100%.[99] If we sell it in two years it is 50%. If we sell it in five years it is 20%. If we sell it in 10 years it is 10%. If we sell it in 20 years it is 5%. If we sell it in 25 years it is 4%. Additionally, because there will be costs associated with maintaining the land (also referred to a trade's "carrying costs") our return will actually be lower than I estimated (although I did this for the sake of ease).

---

[98] I would also note just for the sake of interest that a number of notable historical figures were "land speculators". That is to say, they purchased land with the intention of reselling it at a profit. Many of the United States foremost founding fathers, including the great George Washington, were traders of the asset of land. The so called "wealthiest man in Rome", Marcus Licinius Crassus, was also a land speculator, although his trading/investing practices were particularly predatory and nefarious. Andrew Jackson for his part also attained great wealth as a land speculator.

[99] ([Sale Price – Purchase Price] / Purchase Price) x 100%

For instance, we will have to pay tax on the land, we may have to put a barrier on the land to keep would be adverse possessors off of the land, we may have to pay landscapers to keep the land looking attractive for potential buyers, etc.

As you can see, unlike investing, where additional time exposure increases our annualized return, trading is the opposite. The longer you are exposed from a duration perspective the faster the value of your trade erodes. Said another way, time will decrease annualized return of a trade all other things being equal. As you will also notice, additional time added to the trading process is unkind to our return. That is to say, just as investing enjoys compound growth, the loss of time in trading causes exponential decay to our return.[100] Beyond the mere time component, additional duration in a trade also exposes one to a host of speculative factors that could affect price that one might not expect (i.e. a pig farm gets built next door and smells so terrible no one wants to spend any time on the property we purchased, a sudden decrease in the spot price of natural gas such that it becomes more cost effective to generate electricity from natural gas plants than to use solar farms, a sudden decrease in government tax breaks to incentivize building windfarms, a sudden tax break to solar farms to incentivize building solar farms over windfarms, an increase in the cost of the materials used to build wind turbines such that it becomes less cost effective to build wind turbines, etc.).

---

[100] This of course assumes that the price also does not increase with time (as it often does because value tends to increase with time), but for the sake of an example, this exhibits the force of decay time will exercise on a trade all things being equal.

The risk of duration in trading, is perhaps most visible in the bond market, where bond traders require additional premium (that is to say, an increase in the interest rate received) if duration is longer, all other things being equal. This is quite evident if we take a look at the "risk-free rate", as discussed earlier. In our prior discussion, I used the 3-month U.S. treasury bill as the "risk-free rate". You may notice that 3 months is not a very long time and thereby (from a trading perspective) doesn't expose one to much in terms of exogenous factors which could change the price of the bond in that time frame. The 10-year treasury, which gives exposure to the same risk as the 3-month, other than duration (that is to say, the credit-worthiness of the U.S. government), is typically higher than the 3-month rate, because, to induce bondholders to purchase 10-year notes as opposed to 3-month bills, the bondholders require additional return to make the purchase attractive. This is also true for a 30-year treasury, which gives the noteholder exposure to the credit worthiness of the U.S. federal government for 30 years. The 3-month rate will typically be the lower than the 10 year, and the 10 year will typically be lower than the 30 year (all because of the premium related to duration).

Somewhat unfortunately, at the time I am writing this book, I cannot use a real-world example by listing the various current rates, because the yield curve is partially "inverted". That is to say the current 3-month treasury rate is actually lower than the 10-year rate. On the positive side, this gives me an excuse to briefly discuss "yield inversion" and what it means.

Generally speaking, as we've just discussed the 3-month, 10-year and 30-year treasuries all have the same underlying credit risk (i.e. U.S. government default risk). However, their interest rates (or rates of return) vary based on duration. That is to say, additional duration, is an additional risk and therefore requires increasing compensatory premium to induce demand. However, during the end of economic cycles, some bondholders tend to become pessimistic that the growth phase of an economic or business cycle is going to end. The belief therefore is that generally speaking, most markets (typically focused on the equity market which is the most risky, but middle of the continuum bonds as well) will underperform in the coming years (as we already mentioned typically over a period of 3 years). Said another way, if the growth phase of the entire economy is ending, it is likely that the prospect of additional return or growth will be limited relative to the probability a principal loss will be suffered (said yet another way, the asymmetry of risk is no longer in favor of the investor). As a result, some savvy investors, who recognize the asymmetry of risk has flipped (assuming the asymmetry of risk as actually flipped), become pessimistic and believe that the only credit-risk worth taking is the credit-worthiness of the U.S. government (which is generally believed to be unlikely to become insolvent). As a result, the 10-year treasury note (and depending on how badly the economic recession is expected to be sometimes the 30-year treasury), enjoys higher demand than the short term 3-month T-bill (despite the increased duration risk in the 10-year). The increase in demand pushes up the purchase price (as demand does) and because we know the coupon rate on a bond stays the same, the corresponding yield to maturity falls (because you pay more than par value or more than the face value for the income or interest rate that will be received on the face amount). As of today[101], the yield on the 3-month T-Bill is 2.13%, the 10-year treasury note rate is 2.035% and the 30-year treasury is 2.543%, which if historic correlation is to be believed indicates an economic recession imminent in the next 6-12 months.

It is important to note however, that the 3-month T-Bill is largely pegged to the Federal Funds overnight depositary rate (as discussed earlier) and therefore an inversion can occur if the Federal Reserve sets (or more cynically said, manipulates), the 3-month T-Bill to be above or below where the market would otherwise naturally price the T-Bill. This is usually done to incentivize a type of investment behavior deemed desirable for expanding economic conditions. As you might expect, however, this tends to exacerbate and not solve the underlying lack of sustainable economic growth (that is to say, a shot of morphine isn't going to save the patient, it is just going to make it feel better, until they die), and Federal Reserve action of lowering interest rates to induce additional credit (i.e. "loosening" or "easing" monetary policy) tends to be a fairly reliable indicator of a pending economic recession.[102]

---

[101] June 21, 2019

[102] Additionally, an "inversion" in the yield curve as an indicator of recession tends to have a self-fulling prophecy component, because of the effect an inversion in the yield curve tends to have on investment and corporate banking, which are at their simplest arbitrage businesses. Generally speaking, investment banks and corporate lenders make money by borrowing short-term and lending long-term. That is to say, most investment banking operations work by borrowing money at the "risk-free" rate from the larger bank's central treasury (typically LIBOR or the Fed Funds Rate) and lending it to clients at the "market rate" for the type of loan being given (typically LIBOR or the Fed Funds Rate plus some risk-premium). Because the short-term risk-

free rate is typically cheaper than the longer-term rate (because of the risk of duration), the investment banking division typically borrows at the shortest term rate possible (and rolls it monthly or quarterly depending on whether a one-month or three-month rate was selected) because this increases the "spread" during the life of the loan (i.e. they buy the cheapest loan available and sell the most expensive loan they can within risk guidelines, to pocket as much spread as possible). Loans to clients tend to be for 5 to 10 year periods (most typically 7 years) and as a result, the investment banking division gets the benefit of the risk-premium and additional duration in the spread. As you might expect, if the yield curve inverts, it destroys this arbitrage of risk and duration, by making the cost of borrowing to the investment banking division higher relative to the rate that can be demanded on the loan in the market, thereby decreasing the "spread" (that is to say, because the "market rate" is typically a risk-premium on top of the risk-free rate of shortest duration, the inversion reduces this duration premium). Depending on the severity of the inversion, the spread could be reduced such that the central decision makers at the bank, feel that the risk being taken on is no longer worth the spread received from the loans and the investment banking division is instructed to reduce lending exposure (or at a minimum the banking division tends to underperform their expected revenue metrics). Reducing lending exposure has the effect of restricting credit into the market place (for the clients) and reducing the monetary supply (that is to say, if there are less loans being given there is less purchasing power in the market). Reducing purchasing power in the market, tends to lead to the decline in the value of assets (since the supply of money to purchase assets is decreased) and tends to put pressure on earnings (that is to say, it becomes harder to maintain earnings growth without leverage, particularly late in the growth cycle). A reduction in earnings growth, if severe enough and if experienced across a broad enough segment of the economy can result in a recession. Additionally, the reduction in earnings growth, tends to result in investor fear that the future earnings expected will not materialize, which tends to precipitate a rush out of risk assets (sort of a "run" on assets, as people look to convert back into currency). This tends to result in a large decline in assets prices, which further devalues asset prices (since supply rises relative to demand), which contributes to a negative feed back look that tends to result in a market crash (at its most extreme). Additionally, the reduction in the

Now, despite all of this short-term negativity, you may look back at the annualized rate of returns I mentioned above in our discussion of the windfarm and realize that if you happen to be one of the lucky few who can consistently pull off selling the windfarm in 2 years, you get to enjoy a 50% annualized return, which is far superior than 10% annualized return. After all, the present value of money today is worth more than the future value (although NPV and IRR, would back that out to show whether or not our windfarm was still an attractive investment considering the time value of money) and as such, you may decide trading can be valuable.

Trading can indeed be lucrative (assuming one is good at it, which most aren't)[103], but the danger of course is that it is by its nature speculative and therefore more risky than investing. In the tortoise and the hare race, the tortoise

---

profitability of the bank can (and often) has the effect of decreasing the market value of the bank itself, which can put an otherwise stable bank on shaking footing (and if systemically important can cause wider effects).

[103] Trading is really an exercise in decision-making. To be a successful trader, one must consider the risk of loss, accept that there is a probability that a loss will occur, determine whether the probability is greater a trade will succeed or lose, and then determine whether or not the expected gain of such trade is worth executing given the probability of such loss and the magnitude of such loss. In truth, this analysis is important to almost any life decision, yet few people consider this kind of decision making consciously (and as a result most people are not good decision makers). Many people go their entire life without analyzing the negative repercussions of their conduct and whether those negative repercussions can be endured. Anecdotally, people who recognize the risk of their conduct, accept that such risk can happen, and make an informed decision based on their willingness to accept such loss relative to the potential gain they intend to receive from their conduct tend to be more successful and self-aware individuals.

tends to win in the long run (and traders tend to overestimate how good they are at trading).

In any case, even if one is going to engage in trading, it is important to keep such activity distinct (in both one's mind and one's portfolio of assets) from investing, because trading with one's investments could erode the gains of investing (and destroy the benefit of compounding with time which is the central tenement of investing).

There are two main types of trading: 1) "fundamental" trading and 2) "technical" trading. "Fundamental" trading is characterized by analyzing the underlying data to determine that the current market price is mis-priced from where it should be (either it is too high or too low). As an example, in our windfarm example, we realized that the market value of the greenfield did not account for the demand a windfarm would have for a parcel of land of with its inherent characteristics. "Technical" trading is characterized by analyzing price data (typically linear regression and price acceleration, but sometimes underlying factors like volume as well) to determine if price is likely to move in a direction. Said another way, "fundamental" trading looks at inherent characteristics of an asset to determine if price is likely to move, while trading looks at the mathematical and physical properties of price to determine if price will move. The remainder of this chapter will discuss a few types of "fundamental trading" and their uses, while a later chapter will be devoted to "technical trading".

In my view, there are three main types of "fundamental trading" all of which mirror their investing counterpart: 1) value trading, 2) growth trading, and 3) distressed trading. Fundamental trading tends to mirror its investing counterparts because the underlying data analyzed is the same (it is just interpreted and used with a different goal in mind).

1) Value Trading

The first type of fundamental trading we will discuss is value trading. Value trading is a process by which one analyzes the underlying components of price and inherent value of an asset to determine if price does not accurately reflect the price the market should demand.

The windfarm was an example of "value trading", in that we made a judgment about price based on the inherent characteristics of the asset, which we believed led to the market not appropriately pricing the asset. As you will note by the word "believed", this was an inherently speculative decision to make, albeit a potentially profitable one, and we could have fairly easily been wrong.

Value trading tends to require a pretty robust and fairly consistent dataset, a fairly wide price spread (between what the market price is and what it should be), a fairly short-timeline and a fairly illiquid asset to be successful. It also tends to be very labor intensive.

Beginning first with the dataset, it would be extremely difficult, almost impossible, to be a "value trader" day to day, because the price of an asset day-to-day tends not to fluctuate terribly much (largely because speculation of the value of an enterprise day-to-day tends not to fluctuate terribly much). As a real world example, the enterprise price of your local bagel shop is unlikely to diminish because they didn't have any customers on Tuesday of this week. One day of diminished customer flow, is unlikely to affect the overall value of the enterprise and therefore unlikely to impact the price of the enterprise (even speculatively). Additionally, it is difficult to forecast a change in customer demand based on a dataset as small as one day. However, if for a period of 6-months one saw that demand for bagels was decreasing relative to supply, one might be able to make a guess that the enterprise price is likely to decline in bagel shops in the area and to profit from such guess (by shorting bagel shops for instance), but making this determination would require a fairly large amount of data over a fairly long period of time to make a fairly accurate prediction with any degree of probability to occur. It would also likely take a fair bit of expertise and devotion to understanding the in's and out's of bagel consumers' behavior. It would also take a lot of work in terms of man hours and considerable skill (that is to say a lot of labor, which is a monetary cost in opportunity cost terms). As an example, we didn't just one day wake up and become an expert in windfarm demand. That probably took a considerable amount of diligent training to understand the nature of windfarms, their risks, their ideal layout, etc.

Additionally problematic is the fact that, as we saw in the windfarm example, time works against us in the trading environment. Said another way, time causes exponential annualized return decay. If we aren't fast, our return suffers. For this reason, when trading, it is often important to set a "time stop", that is to say an amount of time for which we believe the trade will work out, after which point we are willing to sell for less (even at a loss) simply to rid ourselves of a trade that is degrading our overall returns.[104]

If we can't be fast (and typically price movement is out of our control so there is no real way to know if we will be fast or not, that is to say it's hard to know if a buyer for a windfarm is going to come along), we need to compensate for this decay. For the most part, the best way to do that is to try and increase the spread between the price we purchased for and the price for which we sell. That is to say, I may be much more willing to accept some time lag, if my expected return will remain high, because the expected return to start with is very large. If my annualized return in year one will be 1000%, I can afford to wait 10 years for the trade to pay off, because after 10 years my annualized return will still be 100% (not accounting for the time value of money, which will make the return a bit less). On the flip side, if the spread is too small and I cannot be sure of the time frame of a trade, it may make sense to just avoid that trade because there is too much time risk.

Typically (but not necessarily), the spread one can achieve is somewhat determined by the nature of the trading market. That is to say, spreads tend to be higher in markets that are relatively "illiquid", because they aren't priced as regularly or as efficiently as an extremely "liquid" market. Said another way, there tends to be a premium associated with "illiquidity" that contributes to an increased spread. Said yet another way, assets which aren't constantly analyzed and priced on a public market (mainly private assets) are more likely to have prices which don't accurately reflect the components of price accurately (underlying value and supply and demand for instance). Because there is less information available continuously,

---

[104] In investing a "time stop" would be perverse, since a properly valued investment should continue to produce cash flow with time adding to returns.

changes in price are more likely to be dramatic. You can think of this also, as being the same degree of price change, but occurring in shorter "jumps" in price. As an example, if I am interested in a public stock, each day I can look on the internet and see its daily change that builds up into its month change that builds up into its three-month change in price. If I am interested in a bagel shop, I will not be able to get any real data on that bagel shop, short of asking the owner, tracking "soft data" or analyzing other similarly situated bagel shops. As a result, even if in reality, the price of the bagel shop changed slightly every day, in practicality when I go to purchase the bagel shop the purchase price will probably exhibit a large jump in price from when it was last sold. Additionally, when I am prepared for a purchase there will be only one seller (there won't be a myriad of sellers all selling the same exact asset like in the public markets) and when I go to sell, there will likely only be a few buyers (which makes the idiosyncratic desires of the seller and the buyer highly relevant in determining the purchase price).

As another example think of selling a home. When I purchase a home, I might purchase that home on the basis of a variety of factors I think contributes to price (its size, its location, its community, etc.). Based on my analysis of those factors, I might decide that the house is being sold for less than it should be. I might then purchase the house. When I turn around and sell the home, it may just so happen that a family who wants to buy that home comes to me looking to buy and that their relative demand (i.e. their desire to live in that community) allows me to sell it to them for a price much higher than I purchased it for, because there are comparatively few other assets similar in nature (maybe only one quite like this house) that they could buy instead.

In economics this is known as “inelastic” v. “elastic” demand and will be discussed further in the next chapter.

As you might expect, however, if there is a vast supply of goods similar in type, the spread will decrease significantly. That is to say, if demand is “perfectly elastic”, then there is a flood of other assets exactly like mine that people could purchase rather than mine. In such a situation, spreads will decrease because purchasers will become unwilling to purchase for a price outside of the market view (because all assets are viewed as the same as all other assets in the market).

Public markets (and equity markets specifically) are generally speaking “perfectly elastic”. That is to say, at any time one, I can buy shares of a company, and if I don’t like those shares, I can immediately exchange them for currency and then use that currency to acquire different shares.

As you might expect from my example above, value trading in the public market from day-to-day is nearly impossible because the market is so liquid. In order to do it effectively, one needs at minimum to have a quarter’s (3 months’ worth of data) generally speaking. Additionally, quarterly earnings tend to be rather volatile, so predicting mis-pricings can be incredibly difficult.[105] Further, because information in the public markets tends to leak out daily

[105] Although in recent times, corporations seek to telegraph any earnings surprises as much as possible to minimize volatility in share price.

(and be forward priced to reflect future expectation), it is incredibly difficult to get "ahead of the news". That is to say, "insider traders" are typically the only ones who know about something before it happens and they typically trade on such information, so that information gets baked into the price, before the common investor ever has a chance to make a value judgment on price in the short-term.

Over the long-term, value trading in public markets is possible, although probably inferior to value investing, because the spreads are low (as mentioned) and the time horizon is necessarily pushed out. Most "value traders" tend to consider themselves "macro-traders", that is to say they base their price judgments on macro-economic events that are likely to cause large price disruptions.[106] Additionally, to make any real money, a macro-trader will have to continuously root for large movements in price in order to make up for the time spent sitting in a trade. As you might expect, by their nature large disruptive movements in price are typically fairly rare, so value trading tends to involve taking a long-term view about something quite dramatic (i.e. like betting on a full-scale economic melt-down or currency crisis).

Interestingly, many value investors, feel that "value trading" is a perversion of their craft and tend to view it with some disdain. In some ways their view is valid, because for most people time would be better spent, using all of that effort and data to invest wisely and grow with

[106] Many macro-traders will also focus on commodities or currencies, because the underlying forces affecting price (like supply and demand and global political interactions) tend to be more rational and measurable than the earnings fluctuations experienced by corporate enterprises.

time (to be the tortoise and grow consistently with the benefit of compounding, rather than the hare seeking the big-return quickly but racing the exponential decay of return caused by time). There is some truth to this (and this is certainly the case for most people), although there are some people who naturally are outliers and trade quite successfully over the course of their careers.

To be sure, however, one should always avoid someone who tells you they are a "value investor" and then begins telling you about the way they time their "investments" or "sell at a profit". This individual is a trader whether they know it or not (and probably a bad one since they don't even know what they are doing by definition).

For my own part, in considering the merit of "value trading", I tend to bifurcate the analysis into liquid and illiquid markets.

As alluded to earlier, value trading can be performed quite successfully in illiquid markets because information is generally less widespread and demand for assets is generally less elastic (typically this occurs in private markets rather than public markets, because private markets tend to be illiquid markets since there are fewer buyers and sellers generally speaking). That is to say, by cultivating a dataset (of soft-data or cashflow) on illiquid assets (like a bagel shops or doctors' offices), traders can effectively determine over a designated period of time whether there is a reasonable expectation of price appreciation (and sufficient buyers in the market) such that the purchased asset can be sold at a higher price to produce profit.[107]

In liquid markets, however, I tend to find value trading to be an ineffective method of trading. That is to say, while it can be done, it tends to have to be done over a long-time period and involve a dramatic event, the end result of which tends to be high-risk (albeit high-reward) trading. It also tends to be somewhat limiting in that one tends to have to focus on a particular asset type and get to know the ins-and-outs of such asset very intimately to perform successfully over time (which requires a lot of effort and skill, all at the risk of speculative loss). I also have tended to find that value traders in liquid markets have inferior performance to technical traders (mostly because of the nature of information flow and pricing data to be discussed in later chapters) and therefore personally consider it a fairly ineffective way to trade. It is akin to high stakes gambling (although in the case of most fund managers, bank-rolled by their clients), some people are good, some people are bad, usually the house wins in the end.[108]

---

[107] This is a strategy typical used in private equity, although it is often conflated as "investing", when it is in fact trading. As we know, private equity investing would involve purchasing a private asset with the expectation of receiving cashflow, equal to a designated rate of return over time. However, because private equity tend to aggregate capital into "funds", which have a designated life of approximately 10 years and then allocate capital with a 10 year time horizon, at the end of which the fund will be liquidated with the capital (and any profit) being returned to investors, all private equity tends to have a component of buying and selling, which thereby subjects funds to the "time decay" and "price appreciation" characteristics which are the hallmarks of "trading" rather than "investing". That is not to say, all private equity is trading, it is just particularly important to determine the strategy a private equity fund is using and to evaluate this with a focus on the effect of time and how the "gain" is achieved, to determine whether one is an investor or a "trader".

[108] Similar to high-stakes gambling, it also tends to be more effective,

The exception to my view in the liquid markets is highly experienced bond traders (strategic bond traders that is, not "market-making" bond traders), commodities traders and currency traders. Bonds by their nature have the income they will provide which is "fixed" at the time of issuance (thus the name "fixed income") and as such, a trader does not need to worry about volatility in underlying value (which in equities tends to be the most volatile and largest price impacting event). Because of this (and as you will recall from our prior discussion), the only factors left to determine bond price tends to be risk of loss of principal and certainty of cash flow. As we already know, this is really a way of saying, bonds price according to their relative risk to the risk-free rate. Thus, as a bond trader, if you are particularly observant and mathematically inclined (most successful strategic bond traders have a background in theoretical mathematics or physics, engineering or another math intensive natural science), you can generate significant trading returns by being aware of movement in the risk-free rate and exogenous factors which are likely to impact the solvency or liquidity of the underlying asset which issued the bond. This can be done reasonably well, in my view, with appropriate temperament and skill, which is typically reflected in the general consensus view that

---

to keep ones chips off of the table and unexposed until some big opportunity presents itself and then to enter positions with extreme conviction. If one is correct, the trader wins big and walks away with a large pay-out. For most people this is not a conceptually acceptable form of "work", in that there isn't a set determinable task each day that needs to be achieved and as such, many people who seek to value trade bleed cash entering inferior trades rather than waiting for a large price movement, the same way an inexperienced poker player might bleed chips betting small on mediocre hands rather than going all-in with pocket aces.

bond traders generally tend to be "smarter" than equity traders.[109]

Similarly, commodity prices tend to be most influenced by supply and demand forces which can be forecast with some effectiveness by individuals who are intimately connected with the price forces that effect the underlying commodities. That is to say, certain farmers tend to be extremely good at futures trading in their area of expertise.[110]

Similarly, currency prices tend to be most effected by relative deficits and surpluses contained in the current account of countries relative to their largest trading partners. As a result, if a "macro-trader" has a strong sense of political stability in various nations, the reserve system of various nations, and an understanding of the trading relationship of various nations, a currency trader can effectively trade based on what they view as mis-pricing of yet to occur political, social or trading events.

---

[109] It is sometimes said that the bond market has a PhD and the equity market has a high school diploma. My view is that bonds, because of their fixed income, are inherently easier to trade because the number of factors that need to be considered to trade them effectively are rooted in mathematical properties that can be understood, if one has the proper analytical training and is a particularly observant human. Colloquially, though bond traders tend to be more educated than equity traders (and more cerebral). There also tends to be fewer "retail" buyers of bonds than equity (although many retail buyers have large exposure to bonds through various pension funds, benefit plans, etc. of which they may or may not be aware).

[110] Similarly, energy marketers and producers tend to be particularly good at understanding supply and demand forces in certain energy related commodity prices.

Generally speaking however, I would say that most people will not be good at value trading and would be much better served to return to the chapter on investing since it is much easier and more stable to have the benefit of time and compounding on your side than working against you (that is to improve rather than destroy your rate of return).

2) Growth Trading

The second type of fundamental trading we will discuss is "growth trading". Growth trading is similar to growth investing, except the main purpose is price appreciation. Said another way, growth trading involves allocating capital or purchasing an interest in an early life-cycle asset with the expectation that the purchase price of the asset will increase as it approaches maturity. That is to say, rather than enjoy the robust future cash flow of an enterprise, once an enterprise reaches maturity the investor "cashes out" (typically by selling to someone else or making an "initial public offering" or "IPO" which would list the asset on the public market and sell the asset to the general public, i.e. the investors who buy public companies).[111]

Much like "growth investing", "growth trading" is based on an understanding of the exponential growth

[111] This is the fundamental reason IPOs tend to be priced too high (because people who understand and have calculated the value of an enterprise are attempting to squeeze as much price benefit out of it). This is also why generally it is a bad idea to buy an IPO (because by their nature their overpriced). Also, interestingly IPOs tend to flood the market when the market is generally overpriced, because early growth investors tend to realize they will get a higher price in the public market (which is less based on rational math calculations and more on public opinion) than they will by selling in the private market.

prospect of the lifecycle of a productive asset (as a result of compounding value). The difference of course, is that with growth trading the focus is buying for a cheap price (relative to the stake in the enterprise received) and then reselling at as high a price as possible (rather than the receipt of future cashflows resulting from the growth cycle). Fundamentally though, the strategy is based on the understanding that an asset is priced more cheaply early in its life than it is as it approaches maturity (because the underlying value of the asset should compound during its lifecycle), just like the strategy for "growth investing".

However, because the strategy is to buy, appreciate in price and then to sell (rather than accept cashflow over time), the passage of time has a decaying effect on the rate of return (unlike growth investing, in which the rate of return, would increase as additional cashflows are received over time). Thus, with growth trading it is important to sell as quickly as possible to minimize time decay. Generally speaking, "growth trading" requires between 1-10 years, because the natural growth phase of the average business is approximately 10 years. If a time horizon is going to be as long as 10 years, a minimum amount of growth (usually a substantial amount of growth) will be required to make up for the time decay resulting from holding the asset for such a long time period (but can typically be achieved because of the exponential growth prospect of so called "growth companies").

3) Distressed Trading

The third type of fundamental trading is "distressed trading". Distressed trading can take a number of forms, but the most common are "flipping" and "raiding".

We will begin first with “flipping”. Similar to “distressed investing”, in “flipping”, a trader purchases an asset which has endured a distress event with the expectation that the distress event is temporary or because of the addition of value the investor will provide (usually termed a “capital infusion”), the asset will survive the distress event and the market price will appreciate once the distress event has passed. At that point, the trader sells the asset at an increased market price and profits the price appreciation. Once again, time decay encourages “flipping” an asset as quickly as possible.

A “capital infusion” is a common tool for the “flipper”, because it is an easy way to increase market value typically. A “capital infusion” is a “short-term” investment in an asset, which one expects to be reflected (typically in an amount greater than the “short-term” investment) in increased market price. It is quite literally injecting value into an underlying business with the intention of (at least in the short-term), causing the asset to survive the distress event and juicing the price so the distressed investor can realize a gain in price appreciation. By way of example, if a business enterprise is having a short-term liquidity issue, its market price may drop because investors may fear that there is potential for insolvency and therefore loss of principal investment. Seeing this, a “flipper” or “distressed trader”, might come in and agree to buy a large stake in equity with the expectation that the cash received from the sale of equity will be used by the enterprise to solve the liquidity issue. When the liquidity issue is solved, investors will be more certain about the prospect of future cashflows from the enterprise (which aside from the short-term liquidity issue is healthy), which will make the asset a more attractive investment, which will increase the market price of that asset.[112]

This same "capital infusion" strategy is also commonly seen in "house flipping", where it is termed a "renovation". In house flipping, a distressed house (i.e. a home in disrepair or that has been seized in bankruptcy) is typically sold for below market value, because it is in an undesirable or uninhabitable state. A "house flipper" will purchase this house below market, spend money to "renovate" or fix the house such that the market value of the house will increase (either back to its fair market price or above it), and then will resell the home. Because a house is a physical asset with inherent attributes (and not a financial asset, which just exists on paper), just giving cash to a house, will not improve its market value (that is to say, technically you cannot give it a "capital infusion"). However, by spending money to improve its inherent characteristics and underlying value, the market price typically appreciates in excess of the capital "invested" into the home in the form of labor and materials (so in effect it operates the same as a "capital infusion").

---

[112] This was another strategy used by the U.S. federal government during the financial crisis. Many systemically important financial institutions were given cash in exchange for preferred equity in their enterprise. This permitted the enterprises to solve their liquidity issues (when no other traders would because it was seen as too risky a trade) and when the liquidity issues were resolved and investors began re-investing (whether because the businesses were healthy again or because they believed the federal government wouldn't permit failure if government capital was at stake) the government sold down these preferred equity positions (at a healthy profit in most cases). However, unlike a distressed trader, the government probably did not have an interest in turning a profit (rather the intention was to prevent widespread social discord resulting from the failure of one of these major institutions), although they profited all the same.

To be sure, a "capital infusion" is not the only tool distressed investors use. As an example, if I were a distressed bond investor and I believe that a distress event for an asset is only temporary, I might seek to purchase senior secured bonds for such asset at a discount, for which I will receive a profit, if the enterprise survives the distress event and the bonds again begin trading at par. At such point, I would sell the bonds at a profit (because the risk of loss of future cash flow will have diminished and the discount will diminish as the bonds are repriced). However, as a senior secured bond investor, I might feel secure knowing that even if the underlying asset does fail, as a senior secured bond holder, the value of collateral is greater than the value of the principal I spend to purchase the bond, because it has been sold at such great a discount. In this scenario, I would not be incentivized to give additional capital to help the business survive, because if it survives I profit and if it fails I also profit (thus any "capital infusion" would only serve to increase my risk of loss and diminish my rate of return).

The second form of distressed trading we will discuss is called "raiding". Raiding is a process by which a distressed trader seeks to profit by realizing the difference between underlying value and market price that sometimes exists in distressed assets. People use different terms to label this process, but I generally consider this to be "asset raiding", although I admit it takes different forms in different contexts.

In our prior bond example, we actually used a form of raiding as a sort of back-stop against value loss in that we were comfortable that if the issuer failed we could receive the value of the principal of our bond by seizing collateral. Picking up on this example, if I purchased bonds at a discount with the intention of forcing the distressed enterprise into bankruptcy (i.e. with the expectation the issuer will default and I will be able to push them into insolvency) knowing that the underlying collateral value is such that the value I will be able to seize exceeds the discount for which I purchased the bonds, I am engaged in a form of "raiding". That is to say, my goal is not for the enterprise to survive, my interests are actually that the enterprise will be killed and I will be able to profit by seizing a portion of its underlying assets as collateral and when I sell the collateral I seize into the market, I will realize a profit (by pocketing the spread between the underlying asset value and the market price of the debt I purchased).

The most dramatic form of "raiding" is known as "corporate raiding". "Corporate raiding" is a strategy in which a distressed trader calculates that the price for which one would have to purchase an enterprise is less than the price for which one could sell the underlying assets the enterprise owns. Said another way, the price of the enterprise is less than its "book value" (i.e. the price-to-book ratio is less than 1). Because of this, the "corporate raider", purchases a controlling interest in the enterprise (a controlling interest will need to be purchased so that the corporate raider can direct the management of the business to act in the interest of the corporate raider rather than in the best interest of the business's survival[113]). If the

[113] Typically, to acquire a controlling interest in an enterprise a premium over the market price must be paid, because there is additional value to being able to own and control and enterprise in excess of being able to just own a passive interest in an enterprise. Typically, an enterprise's existing shareholders and management (who

corporate raider is able to capture a controlling interest in the enterprise, the raider directs management to sell off all assets of value and distribute the sale proceeds as a dividend to the shareholders. When this is complete, the corporate raider should have received value in excess of the purchase price of shares (because the sale of each underlying asset in the market, when all assets have been sold should be in excess to the price paid, the spread between the two thereby resulting in a profit).

Another form of raiding which you may be familiar is "value stripping". As an example, if my friend is selling his 15 year old car that has no real market value (that is to say he can no longer sell it for its value as a means of transportation), I may offer to purchase that car for a significant discount (say $100 for example). I may then take the car to a shop where the shop will break the car down into its component parts and purchase the spare parts from me (or the metal for melting, etc.). If I receive more than $100 for the sale of each of these spare parts, I will net a profit, because the underlying component assets, exceeded the value of the overall productive asset (because the productive asset no longer had the capacity for producing in line with market expectations).[114]

---

tend to believe in the enterprise) resist being taken over by an outside shareholder whose intentions they do not trust and the attempted purchase of control becomes contested in what's known as a "hostile takeover".

[114] As an extreme example, this is also the mentality behind boosting cars and "chop shops". If I steal a car, the monetary price of acquiring the car is zero (although the legal price is high if I am caught, that is to say I will have my freedom revoked). If I take the car to a chop shop, and it is cut to pieces and sold for parts, I pocket any value I get (over $0) for those parts (and the likelihood of my being caught diminishes because it is harder to find a cars stripped down parts than it is to find

While "raiding" can be very lucrative, it is usually considered to be a hostile activity (and generally looked down upon by society). As such, it has been somewhat disincentivized by society and many legal strategies (like the "poison pill" for instance) have been developed overtime to give management and existing shareholders tools to fight off potential "hostile takeovers".[115]

Generally speaking though, if a trader realizes the purchase price of an asset is less than the price of that assets component parts (or in our bond example that collateral exceeds the bond price and you are able to extract the value from the collateral relatively easily), it makes economic sense to purchase the asset, sell the underlying components and pocket the spread.

For all distressed trading, time, once again, has a decaying effect on the rate of return (as does any carrying costs of owning the asset), so distressed trading needs to be conducted as quickly as possible (for as large a spread as possible, although the spread will probably be somewhat set by the market and the discount rate). Additionally, the carrying costs of holding the asset will decrease the rate of return (as will any capital infusions made), so distressed

---

the whole car, if I had tried to resell it).

[115] To be sure, however, there are still a number of investment companies engaged in "raiding" activity quite profitably (although it is typically rebranded as "corporate activism"). It also tends not to proceed in such an openly hostile process of selling a corporation for parts, but rather tends to involve the issuance of some form of junk or high yield bond, such that the equity holder can "dividend recap" or "dividend recapitalization" any residual value out of the enterprise and then collapse under its debt load. (A "dividend recap" is a process by which an enterprise incurs new debt and distributes the proceeds of such debt to equity holders as a special dividend.)

investing typically requires fairly precise mathematical calculations to do effectively (although not particularly complex ones).

4) Front-Running

The fourth type of fundamental trading we will discuss is known as "front-running". There are a number of forms of front-running, but all of the strategies follow the same basic strategy, mainly purchasing an asset at a price, which a trader believes will appreciate in value, because another (typically larger) investor or trader (or group of investors or traders) is/are likely to purchase the asset in such large volume that price is likely to increase (or desires to purchase the asset to such degree that they will pay a premium to make such purpose).[116] As an example, insider trading, high-speed trading and volume trading are all forms of "front-running".

a. Insider Trading

Beginning first with "insider trading", insider trading is a form of trading in which one cultivates an outlet of information which provides the trader with price sensitive information (i.e. information which is likely to

---

[116] Making a purchase in high volume, can create a short-term supply shortage, which causes a rapid, but short-lived price increase. For instance, if I went into a marketplace and attempted to buy all of the rice in the market, the rice seller might be surprised by this and increase the price (usually in proportion to each additional unit I purchase as the supply becomes more scarce), because the seller knows that once he sells all of his rice he will have no more left to sell to any additional customers. Thought of another way, a short-term spike in demand for a product with a set short-term supply can cause a momentary "supply crisis" (or "liquidity crisis") in that product which causes price to rise.

cause a change in the price of an asset) before the information is released to the public. Once the trader receives the information (but before the public has received such information), the trader determines whether they believe the information will positively or negatively impact the price of an asset and then the trader purchases the asset if it expects the asset to appreciate in price because of a positive reaction by the public to the information when it is released or conversely sells an asset prior to a price drop resulting from the release of negative information. Because insider trading disproportionally benefits corporate insiders at the expense of "retail investors" (or people who do not have jobs in upper management in corporations who are constantly in a position to know information before others), insider trading has been made illegal for assets which are "securities" (as defined by the Securities and Exchange Commission or SEC).[117] In essence, "insider-trading" is trading ahead of information; information which will have an effect on a factor that causes the market to reprice an asset.

While typically viewed as "cheating" at the game of trading, insider trading for many years was not considered illegal and was in fact considered a corporate perk of rising to the level of upper management in a large corporation. Additionally, in modern times, in real estate (or any other asset which are not a "securities" within the SEC definition) where insider trading is not illegal, one can quite effectively trade by finding an informational outlet that allows one to be aware of price sensitive information before it becomes general public knowledge.

---

[117] It should be noted that insider trading is not illegal for members of Congress.

b. "High-Speed Trading"

High speed trading is a process by which, a trader collects data about the size of a trade order being placed on an asset, typically on a public stock exchange, with the intention of taking a position in the asset, before the large trade is executed, and pocketing the spread of the increased price that results from the short-term supply shock of the large trade being executed in the marketplace. Typically (because of the electronic nature of stock exchanges in modern times), high speed trading requires high-speed cables and infrastructure linked to a stock-exchange such that price data can be received and processed by an algorithm with speed sufficient to make a trading decision (within milliseconds typically) and trade in front of large trading blocks[118] (typically from institutional clients). Because the execution of a large trading block creates a short-term supply shock, it also typically creates a short-term price spike, which if front-run yields a nice profit for the high-speed trader. The high-speed trader then exits the position (usually within a few milliseconds before or after the block has been executed) at a profit. High speed trading is usually conducted at high volumes for

---

[118] Many individuals and institutions who want to purchase an asset desire to purchase the entire share of assets they desire or none at all (known as an "all-or-none" price limit). As you might expect, it would not be desirable to do a series of investment calculations to determine a rate of return, only to only be able to purchase a fractional share of the desired investment, because the market price moves or there are insufficient sellers to supply the full share purchase desired. Typically, this results in the trade being conducted in a "block" (or "block trading"). That is to say, a block of shares at a certain supply will be purchased all at once. If there is not a sufficient supply of shares to purchase the full order, the share will not be executed (and the order will wait until such a supply is available in the market).

milliseconds at a time, which can make it a highly effective form of trading (albeit a highly technical one), since the risk of loss is minimal and large volumes can be processed, in extremely short-time frames (which minimizes time-decay to the rate of return). The downside as you might expect is that the spread caused by the short-term price shock of a block trade is typically extremely small (maybe only a few cents on the dollar). However, if done with enough frequency and at high enough volume, this form of trading can be extremely consistent and effective.

As you might also expect, having someone front-run one's trades, leads to a higher purchasing price in most cases (that is to say, if a bunch of people are front-running my trade, the price will be bid up before I can execute my block) which results in a higher average price for the investor. For an institutional client processing huge block orders, this transaction cost can significantly increase the purchase price and thereby reduce the rate of return on investments and trades. As a result, institutional clients have responded in two main ways: 1) through the use of "dark pools" and 2) by averaging into positions using smaller blocks of trades.

"Dark pools" are private stock exchanges that have the same function as public stock exchanges (such as NYSE and Nasdaq) with the exception that orders are executed anonymously. Executing orders anonymously helps institutions and individuals who typically execute high-volume orders to avoid having their trades front-run because those who would seek to front-run these traders typically look to see who a large trade is coming from to determine whether or not a large volume order is likely to be executed. As a result of the proliferation of high-speed trading, "dark pools" have enjoyed significant demand and have gained a great deal of market share from the public stock exchanges (which used to control almost the entire market of public trading).[119]

The second way large institutions and individuals who trade and invest in high-volumes avoid being front-run is by "averaging into positions". That is to say, rather than execute a large block of shares, an investor will break up the block into a series of smaller blocks and execute these smaller blocks over a designated period of time. Doing this, will result in an "average price" of purchase, which is typically lower than executing the large block, because there will be limited incentive to front-run these blocks (since they don't cause short-term supply shocks). The downside to this strategy, is that depending on the time frame used to enter a position, it exposes the investor/trader to natural market price fluctuation over the period of time of entry (although this also has the effect of smoothing and short-term fluctuations that are not in favor of the purchaser or seller).[120]

Before we move on, it should also be noted that many high-speed traders have recognized inherent weaknesses in stock exchange systems, which have resulted in a variety of strategies used to game stock exchange procedures for profit. One such concept is known as "spoofing" in which in order to induce a price increase, a

[119] Ironically because of the lack of transparency many dark pools have been themselves guilty of front-running clients, which is a breach of fiduciary duty and typically results in hefty penalties.

[120] Averaging into a position utilizes the "law of averages" as did our earlier discussion of the topic, however, it only exposes the averaging to a designated (typically fairly short) duration and price movement within that duration.

high-speed trader will take a position, then order additional shares (which the trader has no intention of purchasing) of extremely high volume (higher than can be filled in the time period) in order to induce a price increase (which results from the rapid demand increase and resulting supply shock), executes its position at a profit and then cancels all orders for additional shares. This activity is considered illegal (because of its inherent fraudulent nature and the negative impact it has on the functioning of an exchange and traditional investors/traders), but it is just one of many ways high-speed traders use front-running combined with other strategies to exploit small fluctuations in price.

c) Volume trading

To be clear, the central tenant of all front-running is receiving information before others that indicates there will be an increase in the purchase price (typically from an increased volume of purchasers)[121]. Generally speaking, anytime there is expected to be an increase in the volume of purchasing price will increase (as a result of the increased demand relative to the supply) and as such price will increase. As such, any time an individual seeks to purchase ahead of an increase in volume, they will be engaged in "front-running". That is to say, the trading strategy will be solely based on seeking to jump ahead in line of other buyers who will bid up the price of an asset.

As an example, if a trader learned that a group of parcels of land was likely to be bought by a developer to create a large planned community, purchased a parcel of land in that group and then sought to sell at a higher price, because of the value that particular parcel had as a part of

---

[121] Or vice versa.

the whole to the developer, they would be engaged in front-running.

As another example, if a public stock trader used volume in options purchases on a stock, to make trading decisions about whether a stock was going up or down, they would be "front-running" an expected group of buyers as indicated in the volume of stock options purchased.

Generally speaking, front-running, as a class of trading, tends to be a fairly certain form of trading with a fairly high success rate and occurs typically over a short-time horizon which minimizes time decay. It is also why many corporate insiders and professional traders are tempted (and not infrequently succumb to such temptation) to front-run or insider trade, because of its perception of being both practically easy and lucrative (assuming your information source is accurate).

Derivative Trading

It is important to mention that almost all of the trading strategies discussed can be conducted by purchasing derivative products linked to the performance of underlying assets (rather than purchasing the asset itself). If you are a purchaser of a derivative this can be beneficial because it limits the downside of the risk of loss (since a trader cannot lose more than they purchase the contract for) and increases the potential upside of the potential gain (because the value of the derivative will increase in proportion to the change in asset price of the underlying asset since it is a "mathematical derivative" in the literal sense). The downside is that sellers of derivative contracts tend to price a premium into the price of the derivative which accounts for expected fluctuation in price (which decreases the probability of overcoming the price of the premium paid and therefore the derivative gaining in value based on the underlying asset performance). On the other side of the transaction, a seller (known as an "underwriter") of a derivative contract tends to have limited upside, since the total value the underwriter can receive is the premium (and therefore additional performance in the underlying asset is not captured), at the risk of unlimited downside[122] (since out-performance by the underlying asset beyond the premium received will result in a loss equal to the proportional outperformance of the underlying asset). The benefit of being an underwriter, however, is that premium is received in exchange for the obligation of risk, so if the premium is priced correctly, the probability of the asset performing in excess of the premium should be in the favor of the underwriter and the underwriter receives the benefit of the premium without having to allocate any capital (that is to say they are a seller of a contract, so they receive a price in exchange for that contract, unlike the purchaser who must allocate capital to purchase the contract).

Generally speaking, because the laws of probability tend to favor the underwriter, people tend to like to underwrite derivatives if they have the benefit of the law of averages on their side (because even if they lose a few the total premiums should cancel out the loss). The danger of course, is that if, the derivatives are "uncovered" products and the low probability event is not accounted for (that is to say, the low probability event occurs) there is the possibility of unlimited downside.[123] For large institutions

[122] Provided the derivative product is "uncovered". That is to say, the seller does not own the underlying asset for which it is underwriting the derivative product.

[123] Uncovered derivatives contracts played a significant role in the

who serve as underwriters, if sufficient premiums have not been kept in reserve as a capital buffer to pay out claims, these institutions can find themselves insolvent.

This is not to say purchasing derivatives cannot be valuable or lucrative. Purchasing derivatives can be extremely useful as a hedging tool (as discussed before).[124] For an extremely talented trader it can also be of great benefit, because the trader can speculate and get the benefit of a speculative gain without having to own the underlying asset. The danger of course is that a premium has to be paid upfront for the position (so necessarily more than the true value of the contract at the outset is paid in advance) and such premium will have to be overcome in the eventual gain the derivative enjoys (based an underlying asset performance or underperformance). Additionally, most people just aren't talented traders, so people tend to lose more than they win. If people lose more than they win, they will lose faster as a derivative trader than they will as an underlying asset trader. Of course, on the flip side, a talented trader will make more money faster using derivatives, typically, than by purchasing the underlying asset.

If value investing is the tortoise, derivative traders are the hare on steroids. You can get very rich very fast, but people tend to have inconsistent success (or more often loss) which deprives them of the benefit of compounding

---

1929 financial crisis that resulted in the Great Depression. Credit default swaps and CDOs and other similar derivatives similarly played a significant role in the 2007-2008 global financial crisis.

[124] After all, derivatives were created for the purpose of hedging as an initial matter and that remains their primary function (although a robust and speculative trading market has arisen around their original purpose).

(which is the single greatest tool to growing wealth generally). Some people, however, are exceptional traders (or hedgers) and for them derivative products are great at leveraging their talent.

As a final note, it is important to mention that derivatives tend to experience the worst time decay in terms of tradable assets (since the maturity of their life is set and if they do not gain in value beyond the premium by that preset maturity, they expire worthless typically).[125]

Compounding in Trading

Despite the fact that the inherent nature of trading is that time has the effect of causing exponential decay in the rate of return (unlike investing where time has a compounding effect), it is possible to enjoy the benefits of compounding while trading. The primary way to compound trading profit, is to continually trade the gains received from prior trades. As you might expect, because you can lose on any given trade, this strategy has significant risk associated with it and requires mitigating strategies to avoid sustaining substantial loss.

As an example, let's consider a house flipper, who begins with $200,000 in cash. The house flipper finds a home in bankruptcy selling for $200,000 although the market price of comparable homes in the area is approximately $400,000 (so the house is believed to be trading at a 50% discount). The house flipper views this as an attractive trade and believes after purchasing that the house can be sold within a year. The house flipper

---

[125] As an example therefore, derivatives like stock options are an easy way to see the exponential time decay that results in the trading environment.

purchases the house with the $200,000 and succeeds in flipping the home within the year at a selling price of $400,000 or a $200,000 profit. The house flipper now has $400,000 in cash (or a 100% rate of return for the year). The house flipper, then finds two homes in bankruptcy both selling for $200,000 once again at a 50% discount. The house flipper purchases both of these homes and now succeeds in selling both of them for $400,000 that same year. The house flipper now has $800,000 (or a 400% rate of return for the year). As you can see, if the house flipper continues to reinvest all of the profit he receives from his trades, he will compound his return.

The danger of course is that the house flipper can make a bad trade. Let's say that now with his $800,000, the house flipper decides to purchase four homes out of bankruptcy each of which is selling for $200,000 (which represents a 50% discount from the market price). However, after making this purchase the prices of homes drops in the community in which the homes were purchased and the market price of the homes is now only $100,000 (if a seller can find a buyer at all). The trader recognizing that holding the assets will erode his gains with time and that the carrying costs of holding four homes will be significant sells at the new market price of $100,000 or at a 50% loss on each trade. The trader now has $400,000 (or a 100% return for the year).

As can clearly be seen from the example, the trader on each trade has the risk of the loss of its principal on each trade. As such, using one's gains in additional trades can increase the rate of return, but also risks the loss of those gains as well. Additionally, time is always acting against the trader, so for instance if the homes sold for $100,000 couldn't be sold for a full year after the trade was entered (the traders annualized return would be 50% rather than the 100% reported, although the cash on cash return would still be 100% overall).

Thus, to compound, one must be a talented trader (that is to say, one must win more than they lose, in a magnitude in which the amount gained exceeds trading losses) and one must make a risk allocation of how much gains need to be retained and how much gains can be used to make additional trades in order to generate the desired rate of return. Additionally, because time is always decaying the rate of return, the trader needs to be aware of time as allowing a trade to linger will result in erosion of the annualized rate of return.[126]

As an example, if we consider our house flipper and assume that rather than make his initial winning trades over a one-year period, those same trades were made over a ten-year period, our trader's annualized rate of return would go from 400% to 40%.

Trading's Fundamental Attributes

As can be seen, the primary attributes of trading are the element of time decay, price appreciation and the flow

---

[126] Most traders use "price stops" to avoid allowing a bad trade to erode gains too dramatically. Thus, if price begins to decline beyond a certain level, a trader will close a position to avoid a risk of loss to great that would erode the return of the overall trading portfolio. However, comparatively fewer traders use "time stops" that is to say, a time period after which the trader will close a trade that isn't performing or has not yet performed, because the time it is taking to complete the trade is lingering (doing so would often enhance returns because it would avoid time decay, but this is often overlooked by all, but the most talented traders).

of information. Of these, time decay is probably the most significant reason investing tends to be superior to trading over a long-term time horizon.[127] Although trading gains are likely to exceed investing gains in the short-term, over a long time-horizon the benefit of compounding with time is advantageous to return decaying with time. With that said however, it is possible to compound trading gains, but must be done so with a framework for controlling risk to do so effectively over-time.

It should also be noted that unlike investing, where buying an asset at a time at which it is "under-valued" will result in greater return over time, for the trader it matters only that price appreciates after the purchase of the asset has been made. Price appreciation can occur regardless of whether an asset is priced relatively "cheaply" or "expensively". Said another way, for the trader, "prices are never too high to begin buying or too low to begin selling"[128], while for the investor buying assets when prices are high and selling assets when prices are low would significantly diminish returns over time.[129]

---

[127] It also tends to be the reason investors tend to generally be less emotionally taxed than traders. Racing time tends to be a fairly stressful position to be in as a human instinctively, whereas having time on one side tends to be stress reducing for most individuals.

[128] Quotation attributed to Jesse Livermore.

[129] This fact highlights the difference in the paradigms between investing and trading. It is also a fact, however, that is often missed by investment advisors and media pundits. It is a very common experience to be told not to sell an investment, because, even though the market is overvalued, the "rally isn't over yet". This represents a conflation of two separate paradigms that are investing and trading. An investor should never concern themselves with a "rally", but rather be focused instead on whether price is "cheap" or "expensive" relative to the assets productive value. Conversely, a "trader" should not concern themselves with the relative expensiveness or cheapness of

an asset (the underlying productive value of the asset itself or even the type of asset), but only with whether a rally is likely to continue or end.

Chapter 17: Liquidity, Elasticity, the Velocity of Information and Why "why" doesn't matter

Whether one is investing or trading, price is an unavoidable fact that must be considered. In fact, price is one of the single most factors in determining the rate of return for investing. Price (and its eventual movement) is the critical factor that determines if a trade generates a return or causes loss (along with the passage of time). For the fundamental trader, decision-making is based on information one has about the current price relative to the expectation of future price movement. The ability to receive such information and rely on such information is imperative to success.

For the fundamental trader, the question therefore becomes whether information in a market is available to the trader in a time frame which allows the trader to take a trading action before any such information is reflected in price.

Generally speaking, whether or not a trader will have sufficient time to act on price-sensitive information is a result of 1) the liquidity of the market, 2) the elasticity of the asset being traded and 3) the velocity of information.

1) The Liquidity of the Market

"Liquidity" is the speed at which an asset or security can be bought or sold at a price. Said another way, liquidity is a word to describe how quickly an asset can be converted into an accepted unit of exchange which can be converted into other assets. This is often dependent on the availability of buyers and sellers in the market at any given time and the stability and transparency of which assets are sold in that market.

As an example, cash is considered the most liquid asset, because cash is a unit of exchange and can be used to purchase a variety of other assets. Similarly, public stocks exchanges tend to be highly liquid, because there are a large quantity of buyers and sellers at any given time, the bid and ask price for any security are typically displayed transparently and updated continuously (so there is no delay in changes in bid-ask and sale prices) and prices are typically fairly stable because most exchanges use "market-makers" which by their nature make purchases and sell shares to facility stable smooth price movement[130]. Conversely, highly regarded art, while demanding a high price at market, is typically highly illiquid, because there are relatively few buyers, and converting the asset into the unit of exchange at an acceptable price will typically require an auction of some kind or a one-on-one negotiation of the sale price.

2) The Elasticity of the Asset

"Price elasticity" of an asset is a measure of the response a change in its supply or demand have on its price. In other words, price elasticity measures the effect changes

---

[130] "Market-makers" typically accomplish this by making purchases at the bid price and selling it at the nearest sell price, thus pocketing any spread between the bid and sell price, while also increasing the speed of which transactions are processed (since there need not be any negotiation between buyer and seller) and reducing the spread between the bid and ask price (by continuously matching bids and asks that are close together to create a range). As a result, typically one can tell if the market for a security is not terribly liquid by evaluating the extent of the spread between bid and ask prices (that is to say, the larger the spread the less liquid the market is).

in the quantity of available assets of the same type has on the price of that asset. Said in the inverse, price elasticity measures the effect changes in price have on the quantity of purchases of an asset. The main determinants of whether price is "elastic" or "inelastic" are the availability of acceptable substitutes to that asset and the degree of which purchase of an asset is "discretionary".

As an example, if the supply of gasoline falls and the price of gasoline rises as a result, consumers are likely to purchase the same amount of gasoline they purchased prior to the price change, because gasoline is necessary to drive one's car to work. The purchase of gasoline is not really "discretionary" in the sense that the purchase is fairly necessary to one's lifestyle (since not driving one's car will require a major change in transportation behavior). Additionally, because there are no major substitutes for gasoline to power one's car, the consumer has no alternative, but to purchase the commodity in the same quantity as before the price change.[131] The price of such an asset is considered "inelastic" because the asset is not discretionary and no suitable substitute exists for the asset, thus consumers continue to purchase the asset in the same quantity regardless of the movement in price.[132]

---

[131] Increasingly electric cars serve as an alternative, but would require a large capital expenditure to avoid, what is most likely, a short-term change in gasoline prices.

[132] Interestingly, however, the consumer will often cut back in discretionary purchases in other areas of one's consumer life, to make up for this increased expense. Thus, certain commonly purchased and inelastic assets' price movements are often tracked by economists and traders to determine whether the demand for discretionary products is likely to fall.

Conversely, if the supply of coffee falls and the price of coffee rises as a result, consumers are likely to seek a different beverage that supplies their need for caffeine (perhaps tea or a soda beverage). The availability of substitutes to coffee are many and the purchase of coffee as an initial matter is discretionary (that is to say, one could forgo coffee drinking entirely without much effect on one's life). As a result, consumers are likely to purchase less coffee if price increases or said another way, demand for the product is likely to decrease (which has the effect of decreasing price down to an equilibrium price). The price of such an asset is considered "elastic" because changes in price effect the quantity or demand for the asset.

Assets that are inelastic enjoy the benefit of demand even when there are price fluctuations (which has the effect of creating a more stable and consistent price, regardless of underlying fluctuations in supply and typically sets a "floor" price or minimum price of the asset proportional to the non-discretionary non-substitutable demand in an environment of oversupply).[133] Assets that are elastic are subject to decreased demand during times of price increases and more prone to consumers seeking alternatives to such asset (which has the effect of creating a more volatile price relative to underlying fluctuations in supply and keeps the

[133] As you might expect, oil and gas tend to experience a floor price based on inelastic demand, as well as manipulation by OPEC and other foreign bodies, which ensure that price is set at a level sufficient to fund the government of nations which depend on oil and gas (or other natural resources) for production in their economy. Although increasingly, as a result of the removal of export restrictions on U.S. oil and the technological advance in extracting oil from shale deposits, the ability of foreign bodies to manipulate the price of oil has diminished in recent times as the U.S. has become a net exporter of oil.

asset at all times at risk of being valueless to consumers if it can be effectively substituted).

Generally speaking, securities in the United States are considered perfectly elastic. That is to say, at any time, there is an oversupply of the potential alternatives one could purchase. Additionally, any public stock can be substituted for another public stock at any time. Thus, generally speaking, purchasers of a public stock will substitute that public stock for another better performing public stock at any given time all things being equal. Additionally, all "investments" or "trades" are inherently "discretionary", that is to say, the purchase of a security is not necessary to daily life and therefore can be entirely avoided if deemed an unattractive purchase.

3) The Velocity of Information

In an environment of perfect elasticity and liquidity, price is continuously reset (typically on a minute by minute basis in U.S. public markets) to reflect all information available at any given time. Said another way, because the asset is easy to substitute and discretionary, the quantity of an asset a purchaser will buy is determined based on the information available to such purchaser as to the relative value of such asset. If information indicates that an asset is no longer valuable, a purchaser can immediately convert the asset into a unit of exchange and substitute the asset with another asset of the same kind, on which there is information indicating that such substitute asset is more valuable than its price reflects. Generally speaking, the net loss of purchasers will be reflected in a decrease in price in the substituted asset and the net gain of purchasers will be reflected by an increase in price in the substitute asset.

In such an environment, the velocity at which information is received is paramount to pricing. Said another way, if information comes out slowly or periodically, price is likely to stay the same for a period of time, until the new information becomes available. When such information becomes available, purchasers will form an opinion on such information and changes in their purchasing or selling behavior will result in a new price of the asset. If information is continuously being produced, price will fluctuate overtime has purchasers and buyers continuously evaluate whether or not to purchase or substitute an asset based on the information available at any given time.

In the U.S. public markets, information on any particular stock is generally available on a daily basis.[134]

Public Markets and the Channel of Information

Most public markets of securities are highly liquid, perfectly elastic and the velocity of information is almost instantaneous. In such an environment, it can be incredibly difficult to be a fundamental trader, because it is extremely difficult to receive and analyze information fast enough to make a decision about a price change before the price change occurs. This is largely a result of the high speed with which information is released and the nature of the release of information, that is to say, the manner in which information is channeled to the general public.

---

[134] Although it should be noted that some securities experience long periods of relatively no price movement, with periodic "shocks" in price based on reporting of certain financial information or soft data. In the U.S. public markets there also tends to be widespread speculation as to price movement on a fairly consistent basis for most securities resulting in continuous price fluctuations.

In public markets the "velocity of information" is extremely fast (that is to say new price-effecting information is constantly available on any given security) and tends to filter first through corporate insiders (because they are either the decision makers whose decisions affect price or they are made aware of price-effecting information before others because their position in the corporate hierarchy makes it available to them first).

Some insiders, recognizing the value having information prior to the public is, seek to profit on this fact by trading ahead of the news (although this is illegal it does happen). Depending on the magnitude of purchasing, price in a security can actually move prior to the price-sensitive information being released to the public.[135] Additionally, when price-sensitive information gets released to the public, it tends to get released through a variety of media outlets (or said another way another set of insiders who potential trade on the price-sensitive information).

When price sensitive information gets released to the public, certain individuals and institutions are by their nature in a position to act faster on such information than others. As an example, high speed traders (who have the infrastructure to process trades at the speed of light) or professional traders (who spend all day monitoring price-sensitive news and making trading decisions) are typically

---

[135] This is admittedly a slightly cynical view, but it does occur with a fair bit of frequency. In fact, monitoring short-term price fluctuations immediately prior to certain financial and soft-data information releases is one of the techniques the Securities and Exchange Commission uses to uncover insider trading activity. It is also quite apparent on some "minute interval" charts right before big news is expected to be released (like earnings calls) as there will be a sudden spike of short-term buying or selling immediately prior to the news.

in a position to act faster than the average investor or trader.

At the end of the information channel is the retail investor or trader. The retail investor or trader will typically become aware of price-sensitive information only after the price movement has occurred. That is to say, the retail investor or trader typically hears the news after the price movement has occurred or said another way hears what "caused" the price change after the price change has occurred.[136]

In short, pricing in public markets tends to occur based on information flow and the main street common man is usually last to know (they in fact will most likely learn of the information after the fact).

As you might expect, for most people, this makes trading on fundamentals almost impossible in a public market over a short-time horizon because price-affecting information is simply not available to these individuals until after price swings have occurred. Trading in this

---

[136] Additionally, pundits will sometimes create a reason to rationalize price fluctuations if an empirical reason does not appear to exist or if the price movement does not seem to match the sentiment one would expect to be conveyed from the reported news. This is a reaction to the fact, media outlets realize people like to know "why" something occurs (it tends to provide a soothing function to the human condition which is inherently somewhat uncertain), so they give are incentivized to give a reason even if one doesn't exist (because that presumably is why people watch the show). This tends to result in widespread speculation (typically inaccurate) by media outlets as to why price is moving on any particular day (even though daily fluctuations could have no real "reason" at all other than someone woke up that day and decided for a variety of personal reasons to execute a large block of shares).

manner will result, in an individual constantly "chasing" the news and will typically not be successful.

This makes trading on fundamentals highly speculative, because in the short-term information is the only factor determining price, price is repriced continuously, and information is restricted through a channel which terminates at the average trader.

As a result, if one wants to trade on fundamentals in a public market, the trader will need to take a long term view, so that such trader has enough data available and enough lag-time in re-pricing such that a judgment can be made regarding the future price of an asset before the change in price occurs. This forces most fundamental traders to have to take a longer-term outlook (since evaluating information overtime and ignoring short-term price fluctuations can still prove profitable if one's evaluation and dataset are accurate), which of course has a negative impact on returns because of the nature of time decay previously discussed.

This is also why, fundamental traders tend to perform better in private markets, which are less liquid than public markets (and velocity of information tends to be slower and less restricted). Because information is received slower and price is unable to react as quickly, there is typically sufficient lag time between the release of information and the change in price for a trader to complete a trading action (and profit from the change in price).[137]

---

[137] Additionally, as already discussed, if the asset is not a security and in a private market, it is typically perfectly legal to cultivate an information source and insider trader. That is to say, to attempt to receive information before it is released to the wider public and reflected in price.

Over longer time horizons, fundamental trading can yield success, although I would caution that it typically causes loss for the common retail investor. Historically, the common retail investor will tend to buy in the middle to end of growth cycle because the common retail investor will generally not trust or become aware of positive news in the market until most other more sophisticated traders are aware of it. In fact, history shows that most retail investors tend to purchase risk assets at the end of a market cycle because that is when productive risk assets tend to reach "all-time highs" and such achievement becomes newsworthy on general news. At this point, common retail investors generally become aware of the fact that an asset could have been profited from and they desire that profit (additionally the mimetic nature of humanity plays a role as those who missed out on the opportunity to invest begin to desire the profit other people have achieved). At this point, the sustainable growth in the productive assets tends to fall away leaving the common retail investor holding the bag when the assets enter a decay phase in their life-cycles. Some fairly sophisticated financial professionals actually use this tendency as a barometer for whether a market-cycle is nearing its end (that is to say when unsophisticated financial people suddenly have an interest in finance it tends to be a sign that a market cycle is ending).[138]

---

[138] Robert Prechter's book "The Socioeconomic Theory of Finance" describes in great detail that markets tend to move in accordance with waves or phases of social mood and that headlines, in fact, tend to follow such mood, such that price movement resulting from changes in social mood tend to lead the headlines. That is to say, Robert Prechter's analysis reveals, among many other interesting things, that news headlines will tend to be most negative or pessimistic after price has already fallen to its bottom and most optimistic when at a market top.

Why "Why" Doesn't Matter

For most fundamental traders, the most important question is "why" something is happening. That is to say, fundamental trading is founded on the belief that by understanding the component factors of price, one can analyze these underlying factors to detect mis-pricing and profit from such mis-pricing.

However, as discussed above, in public markets over a short-time horizon, the answer to the question of "why" is not terribly useful for making a trading decision. The answer to the question of "why" a particular price fluctuation has occurred is inherently backward looking and reactive. The answer to the question "why" does not provide a trader with the ability to make a trading action based on the answer (except perhaps to make a future prognostication on whether such price fluctuation is likely to be sustained or to be short-lived). That is to say, the answer to the question of "why" has no (or at least limited) actionable value as to the event which it explains.

More likely (and admittedly a bit speculatively), I suspect that the fascination with the question of "why" price fluctuation has occurred serves a placating function that allows an investor or trader to rationalize the gain or loss realized from any particular trading decision.[139] That is to say, human nature comes with it a desire to understand why a particular event has occurred. Understanding the underlying cause is generally believed to assist in finding a solution to the problem (if the event is negative) or to assist in causing the event to occur again or recognizing when

139 Financial media outlets profit off of this insatiable demand in the financial world to know why things are happening generally.

such event is likely to occur again (if the event is positive). There is undoubtedly some truth to this desire to understand in empirical sciences.[140] However, in trading (particularly over the short-term) because of the velocity of information and the channels it flows through, relying on one's understanding of "why" is unlikely to result in successful trading, because the trader will always be reactive or "chasing the news".[141]

As a result of the above many fundamentalists believe that it is impossible to trade successfully over a short-time horizon. In fact, it is not uncommon for value investors of significant merit, to completely denounce trading altogether in the same way they might denounce the use of hard drugs or other morally corrupt activity.

I disagree with these fundamentalists, as trading, even over a short-term can be highly lucrative.[142] For

---

[140] I will also admit that over a longer period of time, understanding the nature of markets and how they operate leads to a better trading and investing actions and more accurate recognition of growth phases and market cycles. Not an insignificant portion of this book has been dedicated to understanding the "why" of investing and trading. However, I maintain that using the answer to the question of "why" any particular price movement has occurred, is inherently backward looking and unlikely to result in a positive trading result.

[141] The exception of course being insiders who will have the price sensitive information prior to the price movement, but are prohibited from trading under punishment of U.S. federal law.

[142] While admittedly a bit out of context, I would also note that most people are engaged in some form of trading. Earning a wage is a form of trading (albeit a fairly consistent one). That is to say, one trades time and a skill for a unit of income, while evaluating the probability that that future expected income is likely. In some ways, this is an unfortunate trade wage earners make, since time is perhaps the most important assets any human can hope to possess. Similarly, many professions regularly engage in trading in one form or another

starters, in illiquid markets, fundamental trading is itself a viable trading strategy. While I agree that fundamental trading over a short term is unlikely to succeed in a liquid public market, trading in a liquid public market is far from impossible. A different strategy is simply required.[143]

---

consistently and successfully. Plaintiffs attorneys on contingency trade successful legal arguments for currency. Entrepreneurs trade ideas and a collection of individuals gathered to accomplish such ideas for capital.

[143] I will admit, however, that most people are much more likely to succeed financially by investing rather than trading, because most people tend to lack the required discipline, temperament and foundational mathematics education required to trade a public market effectively.

Chapter 18: Technical Analysis of Price

Before we begin our discussion of "technical analysis", it is useful to make a few preliminary observations. First, almost all of our discussion to follow will have at its base Newtonian law. That is to say, it is primarily a discussion of foundational physics equations on which the natural world is based.[144] Second, while the concepts may seem foreign at first, by nature of living in the natural world, these laws are used every day in extremely common ways. Third, because these laws are, generally speaking, not well understood in the world of finance, they are often perverted and misapplied by the nefarious and/or misinformed.[145] Fourth, it is quite possible, from a visual perspective to conceptualize the same mathematical phenomenon in different ways and as such, sometimes concepts viewed as distinct in fact rely on the same underlying principles. We will endeavor in this chapter to lay bare these underlying principles.

Before engaging in our discussion of foundational principles, it is important to understand that everything that follows is a mathematical (or physics) approach to understanding price. As we know, just looking at price and making decisions is not investing, so we are, by definition, engaged in a discussion of trading. However, I would note that understanding price fluctuations can prove useful to an investor by facilitating the purchase of productive assets when they are "cheap". Regardless of the manner in which one desires to utilize the understanding of price we will

[144] Generally attributed to Sir Isaac Newton.

[145] Not unlike an alchemist's of the middle ages understanding of chemistry. To be clear, the alchemist is to be faulted, but the underlying chemistry is not to be disregarded as untrue.

discuss, it should be noted that for purposes of discussion we will concern ourselves only with "price" and its movement. I would just note that the mathematics we will discuss below can, in truth, be applied to any robust dataset that can be characterized as a "distance" traveled occurring over time (and therefore any object that moves either physically or conceptually).

1) Newtonian Law and Classical Mechanics

You may remember from grade school, that Sir Isaac Newton observed three "laws of motion", which became the basis of "classical mechanics". Classical mechanics, generally speaking, is the use of mathematical methods to describe the motion of "bodies" under the influence of a system of "forces" and is used to describe the motion of macroscopic objects (i.e. objects visible to the naked eye). Said simply classical mechanics uses math to describe motion in the physical, visible world.

Newton's second law of motion (Force = mass x acceleration) serves as the mathematical basis for classical mechanics. When a force is exerted on a mass, it accelerates and is displaced to a new position.[146] The change in position caused by this displacement over an interval of time is known as "motion".[147]

In classical mechanics, the study of motion is separated into statics, dynamics and kinematics, where statics is the study of equilibrium or the forces that act on a

---

[146] The product of the force and displacement is known as "work".

[147] The change in position is observed by an observer from a "frame of reference". However, for our purposes we can assume a pre-Einstein or Galilean relativity, where time is absolute and the observer is at an inertial frame of reference (or not in motion).

body while the object is at rest, dynamics is the study of the forces which cause motion, and kinematics is the study of the implications of the observed motions of objects without regard to the forces causing them to move. In the financial markets, we are concerned with kinematics.[148]

Kinematics is derived from the position of objects over a period of time and is generally described in mathematical terms in "equations of motion". Generally speaking, "equations of motion" are multivariable differential equations, which can be either linear (a system in which the changes in inputs are proportional to changes in outputs) or non-linear (a system where changes in inputs are not proportional to changes in outputs). Price (like most systems in the natural world) is non-linear. Thus, the motion of price is a non-linear multivariable differential equation.

Equations of motion are grouped into two main classifiers for rigid bodies (or bodies that do not exhibit any "deformation" when force acts upon them)[149], translations and rotations; where translations are movements of a rigid body that move every point in a such body by the same distance in a given direction and rotations are movements of a rigid body where a point remains fixed. All rigid body

[148] Since as we have already discussed the number of factors exhibiting force on price in a public market are numerous and inconsistent, particularly over a short-time horizon and we are less interested in determining the answer to the "why" question and more concerned about the question of "where" price is likely to go. Although to be sure both statics and dynamics are relevant to the motion of price (and can be used to varying degrees in the trading context).

[149] Price can be assumed in our equations to have zero deformation. That is to say, we will assume that any form acting on price in a perfectly elastic, liquid public market will move the price.

movements are translations or rotations (or some combination of the two).

For explanatory purposes, we will only concern ourselves with the equations of motion for translation (although the rotation occurring will be apparent in the linear regression discussion).

Generally speaking, the differential equation of motion is a function of position of an object, its velocity, and its acceleration. Velocity is the first time derivative of position. Acceleration is the first time derivative of velocity and the second time derivative of position. We will take each in turn.

a. The Variables

i. Position

In Euclidian geometry (or a two-dimensional plane)[150], the position of a rigid body is defined in relation to a "coordinate system" fixed on an arbitrary reference point in space called the "origin" (typically represented by the value (0, 0)). In cases, where position moves relative to time, the position relative to the origin is typically represented on the "y-axis" or vertical axis of the two-dimensional plane.

ii. Time

In a coordinate system where position is a function of time, time is represented on the "x-axis" or horizontal

[150] It should be noted that physics generally recognizes that geometry occurs in more than a two-dimensional plane, mainly three-dimensions in the macroscopic world and four-dimensions in space-time as described by Einstein's theory of relativity. For our purposes, however, price operates in a two-dimensional plane where price is a vertical plane and time is a horizontal plane.

axis of the two-dimensional plane. In pre-Einstein relativity (or Galilean relativity) time is considered absolute and the same for all observers observing a given event. That is to say, time moves at a set interval (i.e. a constant horizontal force), which is experienced the same by all observers. In the context of the financial markets, we can use pre-Einstein relativity, since our lives on planet Earth in the macroscopic world are subject to absolute time.

iii. Distance and Displacement

In a coordinate system where position is a function of time, position will move relative to the origin. Where position is moving relative to origin, movement of position will be the result of two forces, a "vertical force" (up and down) and the "horizontal force" of time (sideways). As such, position will be represented by a "vector" or a line segment with both magnitude and direction. The magnitude of the line segment will be the aggregation of the forces acting on the rigid body (i.e. price and time) and the direction will be the result of the angle that results from this aggregation of the horizontal and vertical force. Said another way, the aggregation of the vertical force (which for price will be a myriad of underlying forces) and the horizontal force (of time) will result in an angular vector relative to the origin (since the one force will pull the rigid body to the side and the other up, the end result will be that the position will move at an angle relative to the origin in proportion to the magnitude of the upward or downward force relative to the magnitude of the horizontal force).[151]

[151] To calculate the magnitude of the tangential force, one takes the magnitude of the horizontal force and the magnitude of the vertical force and uses these two figures to calculate the hypotenuse (since a horizontal force and a vertical force will always form a "right-

The vector quantity that measures how far the rigid body has moved relative to the origin is known as "displacement".

The scalar quantity (i.e. magnitude only without direction) of the total movement of the rigid body is known as "distance".

b. The Derivatives

In calculus a "derivative" is a measurement of a function's output's sensitivity to changes in its input. Said another way, a "derivative" is a measurement of the "rate of change" of a function. This can be thought of as a fractal, in that, a derivative is an equation inside of a function, that measures the rate of change of that function. The first derivative of a function is a measurement of the "rate of change" of that function. The second derivative of a function is a measurement of the "rate of change" of the "rate of change" of that function (or said another way, the first derivative of the "rate of change" or the first derivative of the first derivative).[152] In calculus the derivative function is considered a "differential equation" of the function whose "rate of change" it measures. Inversely, the function whose "rate of change" is measured is the "integral" of the derivative function.

---

triangle"). The angle will be determined by dividing the vertical force by the hypotenuse and then taking the inverse sine of the product or, alternatively, by dividing the vertical force by the horizontal force and then taking the inverse tangent of the product.

[152] We have already encountered this concept of derivatives in Chapter 12 in our discussion of the rate of change in GDP.

i. Velocity

In classical physics, the "rate of change" or first derivative of the position of a rigid body moving relative to time, is known as "velocity". That is to say, velocity measures how quickly a rigid body's position changes over a period of time. Mathematically, the "average velocity" is defined as the change in position divided by the change in time (or $v(t) = \blacktriangle p / \blacktriangle t$ or $v(t) = (p_2 - p_1) / (t_2 - t_1)$) and is generally used to find the average "speed" of an object between a series of measured points over a time interval. Graphically, average velocity is represented by the slope of a line connecting the positions used in determining the "change in position" over the time interval. However, if position of a rigid body is a "displacement vector", then one can calculate the velocity of the rigid body at any particular time or said another way its "instantaneous velocity" or "instantaneous rate of change". Mathematically, to calculate the "instantaneous rate of change" one "differentiates" the function of displacement using the equation $v(t) = \lim_{\blacktriangle t \to 0} \blacktriangle p / \blacktriangle t$.[153] Graphically, instantaneous velocity is represented by the slope of the tangent line to the graph of the function. The tangent line being the best "linear approximation" of the function at that input value.

[153] Expressed in the inverse, the integral of the velocity function is the displacement function $p(t) = \int v \, dt$.

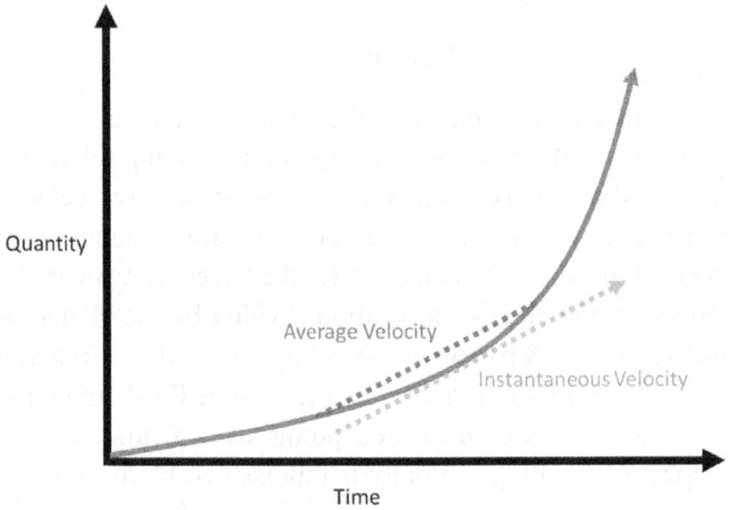

ii. Acceleration

In classical physics (and special relativity), acceleration is the derivative of velocity with respect to time and second derivative of position of a rigid body moving relative to time. That is to say, acceleration measures the change in the velocity of a rigid body's position over time. Mathematically, the "average acceleration" is defined as the change in velocity divided by the change in time (or $a(t) = ▲v / ▲t$ or $a(t) = (v_2 - v_1) / (t_2 - t_1)$). Graphically, the average acceleration can be visualized on a graph of position by observing the angular rotation in multiple average velocity lines drawn. However, if position of a rigid body is a "displacement vector", and one can therefore calculate its "instantaneous velocity" or "instantaneous rate of change", then mathematically, one can calculate the "instantaneous rate of change in velocity" or the "instantaneous velocity" by "differentiating" the function of velocity using the equation $a(t) = \lim_{\blacktriangle t \to 0} \blacktriangle v / \blacktriangle t$ (or expressed in the inverse the integral of the acceleration function is the velocity function $v(t) = \int a\, dt$). Graphically, instantaneous acceleration can be visualized on a graph of position by observing the angular rotation in the slope of the tangent lines of instantaneous acceleration.

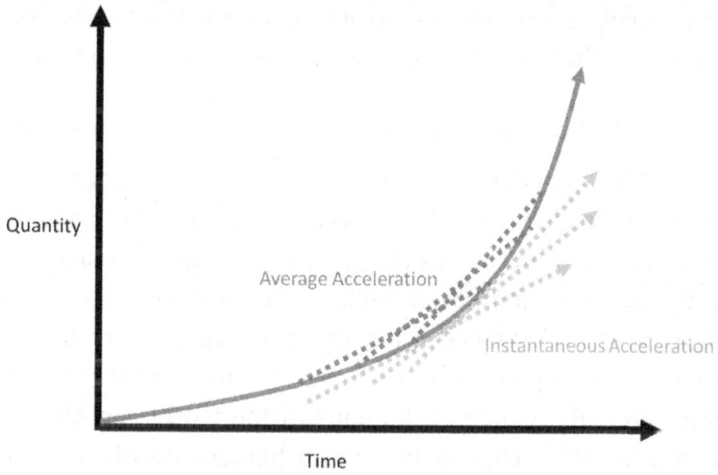

c. Frames of Reference and Einstein Relativity

Position, velocity and acceleration of a rigid body are typically described with respect to an "observer". That is to say, position, velocity and acceleration are "observed" from the position of the observer (as well as any associated motion associated with the observer). This is referred to as a "reference frame". Classical mechanics generally assumes that there are no forces acting on the observer and therefore the observer is not in motion[154] or said another way the observer is in an "inertial frame" of reference.

[154] Or is moving uniformly in a straight line.

This, of course, need not necessarily be the case. Non-inertial reference frames form a central component of Einstein's theory of relativity. The particulars of this will not be discussed, because it is not relevant for our discussion (since a trader has an inertial frame of reference when observing price), but it is worth noting that in a car for instance, velocity of other cars viewed relative to the velocity and acceleration of your car is position, velocity and acceleration viewed from a non-inertial reference frame and therefore follows the laws of Einstein relativity.

2) Price

As previously discussed, price is the amount of "unit of exchange" an individual must exchange to purchase an item of value or asset. Price fluctuates in response to a myriad of factors which exert "force" on price, which displaces price up or down (that is to say, price can go up or down). Price fluctuates over absolute time intervals, which all humans of the world can observe with uniformity (that is to say, all humans on planet earth observe price from an inertial frame of reference).

a. Price is the "position" of a "rigid body" "displaced" from its "origin"

Based on our understanding of price, we can see that if we observe price from our inertial reference frame, we can clearly see that price is nothing more than a "position" of a "rigid body" from its origin. A "rigid body" that is "displaced" by the dynamic forces which continually act upon it in a vertical plane (or said another way price can move either up or down). Additionally, price's position is a "function of time", because the horizontal force of time is always acting on it in absolute terms (in accordance with

Galilean relativity) as time drags everyone on planet Earth into the future at constant intervals. Thus, "price" is a position of a rigid body moving as a result of dynamic forces which cause it to be displaced relative to its origin as a function of time (which can be visualized on an Euclidian plane or "chart").

b. The "Dynamics" of Price

While we are primarily focused for purposes of this discussion on the "kinematics" of price, it is worth pausing, however, to note that the underlying "forces" which act on price are the basis for the "fundamental" analysis we discussed at great length earlier and can be understood as an understanding of the "dynamics" of price. Of the "dynamics" of price, the most important in a perfectly elastic, liquid, public market tends to be the "volume" or the amount of net purchasers or sellers at any given time[155]. That is to say, if there are more purchasers than sellers price will go up and if there are more sellers than buyers price will go down. There are a number of theories (of which Dow Theory is probably the most famous) which rely on analysis of underlying "volume" to determine if a price movement is sustainable or if it will be short-lived. I will admit that understanding underlying dynamics is and can be useful, however, we will not discuss this at length for purposes of this discussion. The reason, I will not, is that price, inherently factors in changes in the net volume of purchasers or sellers (as well as all of the other potential

[155] This discussion of "volume" is really a discussion of "supply" and "demand", which are the central forces which act on price. However, in a liquid, perfectly elastic market, as previously discussed, demand becomes the sole consideration because there is an infinite supply of substitutes. As such, net volume of buyers or sellers (or said another way, demand) is the central force acting on price.

factors that could affect price, including potentially price-sensitive news which has not yet been released to the public and is known only to insiders) and thus, the use of kinematics to analyze price itself tends to provide more useful information regarding price movement in my view (since it potentially prices in information, a trader may not even know exists).

c. Velocity of Price

Because price is mathematically nothing more than the position of a rigid body moving as a function of time, the velocity of price can be measured quite effectively. As can be seen from the math above, either the average price velocity can be measured or the instantaneous price velocity can be measured, using the equations described above.

d. Price Acceleration

Because price is mathematically nothing more than the position of a rigid body moving as a function of time, the acceleration of price (or rate of change of velocity) can also be measured quite effectively. As can be seen from the math above, either the average price acceleration can be measured or the instantaneous price acceleration can be measured, using the equations described above.

e. Linear Regression as an approximation of instantaneous velocity

As you may have noticed, however, it is fairly difficult to calculate velocity and acceleration of price (or really any non-linear multi-variable data set). Fortunately, there is a mathematical way to approximate both velocity and acceleration through the use of statistical analysis. That is, through use of "linear regression".[156]

i. Linear Regression

For any given data set, a linear regression model assumes that the relationship between a dependent variable and an independent variable (and the resulting vector between the two) is linear when modeled with a range of variance (usually termed the "error variable"). Said another way, a linear regression model draws a linear line[157] which best fits a data set after accepting a distribution (or random deviations across a standard accepted variance) of positions.[158] Generally speaking, linear regression is most helpful and accurate when one of the variables (typically the independent variable) is constant.

ii. Linear Regression and Price

Price charted on an Euclidian plane is a dependent variable of time (that is to say it is a function of time). Additionally, time (the independent variable) is a constant. As such, linear regression serves as a suitable tool for determining the "vector" by which price is moving (that is to say for drawing the "hypotenuse" of the vector which results from the horizontal time force and the vertical price force). Additionally, because price tends to be normally distributed (that is to say, price tends to fluctuate in a range), linear regression lines tend to fit charts of price

---

[156] Technically, we will be discussing "polynomial regression", which is a form of "linear regression", but for our purposes the generic label of "linear regression" serves.

[157] According to the algebraic math, $y=mx + b$.

[158] A standard deviation or distribution is often also added to a linear regression line, to show the relative "fit" of the statistical data to the linear model.

fairly accurately.[159] While the math of linear regression can be complex, most computers today can calculate and draw a linear regression line without much effort. Additionally, if all else fails, a linear regression line can be approximated by simply drawing a line through the center of a dataset at a slope that incorporates as much of the datapoints as possible.

iii. Linear Regression and Price Velocity

Because a linear regression line is a vector of the vertical force of price and the horizontal force of time, it is a displacement vector of "position" (not unlike the hypotenuse we calculated in the prior section). As such, the slope of a linear regression line will approximate the slope of the vector of position or said another way, the velocity of price. [160]

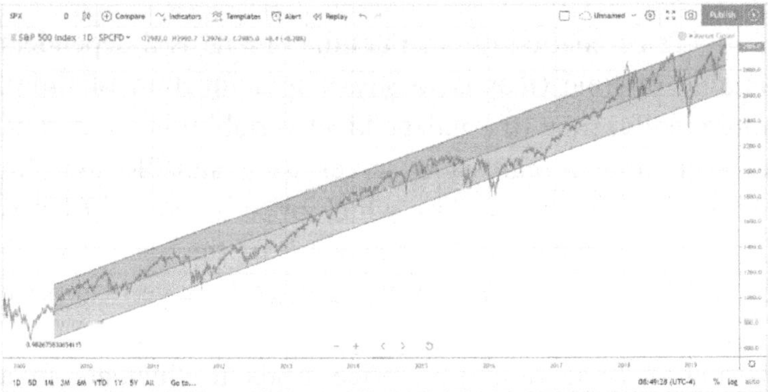

[161]

---

[159] To be sure, the volatility of a security will generally determine whether a linear regression line is useful (because a securities volatility is a measure of its variance or distribution around an "average price").

[160] It should be noted that in my chart, the distribution of price positions falls within a "standard deviation" which is also displayed.

[161] www.tradingview.com

iv. Linear Regression and Price Acceleration

Because the slope of a linear regression line can serve as an approximation of price velocity, changes in the slope of a linear regression line can serve as an approximation of price acceleration.[162]

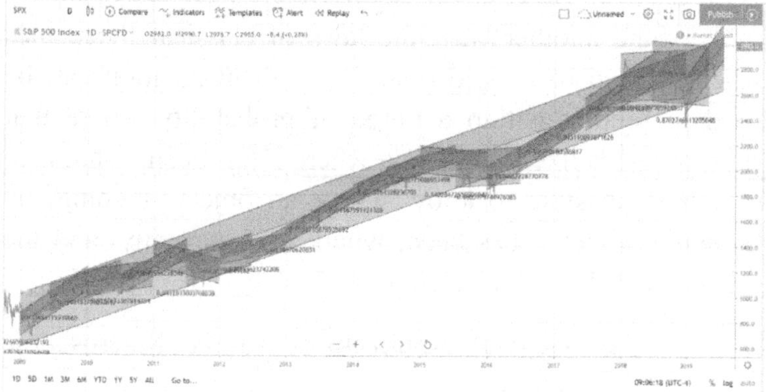

163

3) Determinism and Reversibility

Now that we have laid a foundation for the laws of classical mechanics and how those laws can be applied to price to determine its position, velocity and acceleration, it is important to determine if knowing this information has any useful benefit.

---

[162] It is notable, that the chart of acceleration follows the "S-curve" typically seen in the growth/decay cycle of productive assets described earlier. This is likely due to the fact that growth by nature of compounding, tends to begin linearly, accelerate as compounding begins, steady as compounding continues, and then decline as the mediums for sustaining growth are exceeded, before rolling over to a negative velocity and retreating to an equilibrium (at which point there should theoretically be little to no velocity, exhibited as a flat line).

[163] www.tradingview.com

One of the benefits of the laws of classical mechanics (and the main benefit in the context of price) is that in the macroscopic world, if the present state of an object is known it is possible to predict (within a range of probability) how it is likely to move in the future (known as "determinism") as well as how it has moved in the past (known as "reversibility").[164]

Said another way, the laws of classical mechanics when applied to a rigid object of known position can be used to predict within a range of probability where that rigid object is likely to go and where it has been. That is to say, it is possible to know where an object is going, by knowing where it has been, where it is currently, and the relative speed at which it moves.

a. General Applicability to the Macroscopic World

To be clear, while we will be primarily concerned with price, in the discussion to follow, in the macroscopic world, the determinism and reversibility of classical mechanics permit us to make fairly accurate approximations about almost anything that can be characterized as displacement of a rigid body in motion as a result of dynamic force as a function of time.

i. Determinism in the Virology Lab

By way of example, the first place I recall encountering determinism was in a virology lab, while at university, attempting to track cellular growth of Vero™

[164] It is important to note, that determinism and reversibility are hallmarks of the macroscopic world, while "indeterminism" is the hallmark of the sub-atomic or quantum mechanical world (due in no small part to the Heisenberg principle).

cells. That is to say, linear regression lines drawn through point data of cell growth from day-to-day, was used as an approximation of the growth rate of my laboratory cells and was my primary tool for ensuring I distributed sufficient growth medium to my cells to maintain growth sufficient to conduct virology experiments on said cells (as it is for many scientists).

ii. Determinism in the Car

Additionally, although I was not aware of it, I had also encountered determinism every time I sat in my car and began driving around. That is to say, a general awareness of the angular direction of my rectangularly shaped car, and the velocity of the car, could effectively determine where my car would take me. Additionally, when changing direction, I would need to use the steering wheel to adjust the angular direction of the vehicle to set a new course (and deaccelerate the car to prevent the tangential force caused by the inertial velocity of the car from causing my car to spin out while turning).

iii. Determinism in Sports

Athletes use determinism in a variety of sports to achieve a desired athletic result[165]. By way of example, the angular direction of a golfer's stance, the swing speed of the golfer, and the degree of angle of the club face (as well as the relatively consistent size, weight and shape projectile, i.e. golf ball) can all be used to approximate the flight of the golf ball and its ultimate final position.[166]

---

[165] This is particularly obvious in sports which involve a projectile of some kind, i.e. throwing, swinging or shooting sports.

[166] Interestingly, but somewhat anecdotally, it has long been a priority of wall street firms and trading firms to hire former collegiate athletes

iv. Determinism's Historical Use in Navigation

Historically, determinism and reversibility were commonly used in navigation over land or bodies of water, in a process known as "wayfinding".[167] The classical laws of mechanics used in "wayfinding" are characterized in different ways depending on the strategy and tools used, but typically the simplest form of "wayfinding" has been come to be known as "dead-reckoning". Generally speaking, however, all forms of wayfinding are primarily concerned with predicting future position by orienting oneself relative to a reference point or landmark and being aware of velocity and acceleration to determine distance traveled. Said another way, wayfinding is about "knowing where you are going by knowing where you have been."[168]

b. Dead-Reckoning

Dead reckoning is a process of calculating one's future expected position (or current position) using a reference point, based on knowledge of a prior known

---

or military individuals. Undoubtedly, this is partially due to the apex predatory nature of the environment, but I generally believe that there is also likely a subconscious recognition that athletes instinctively appreciate the concept of probabilistic determinism that made them successful athletes. In more recent times, engineers, physicists and scientists, who are highly familiar with Newtonian calculations have increasingly become staples of wall street and trading firms as well.

167 Interestingly, animals have also been thought to use reversibility and determinism to determine their position in their travels through a process referred to as "path integration". Such inertial-based navigation in animals was first hypothesized by Charles Darwin in the 17th century.

168 The character Maui, voiced by Dwayne "the Rock" Johnson, in the Disney movie Moana.

position (known as the "fix"), together with calculations of estimated speed, elapsed time and angular direction. Said simply, dead reckoning uses angular direction and speed (together velocity) to determine where someone can expect to end up with the passage of time relative to a fixed prior position.

i. Dead-Reckoning in Price

Since we have already established that price (when charted on an Euclidian plane as a function of time) can be characterized with reference to position relative to an origin and consequently changes in price can be measured using calculations of velocity and acceleration (approximated using linear regression), measurement of velocity (which has as a vector component angular direction), together with awareness of any changes in price acceleration, can effectively predict future position (within a range of probability) for an interval of elapsed time. Colloquially, this is typically referred to by traders as the "trend" or, when represented graphically as a line (typically an approximation of a linear regression line), the "trend-line".[169]

[169] Trend-lines tend to have a range between -60° and 60°, because the constant horizontal force of time at 0° drags the -90° or 90° force of price continuously in absolute units into the future, which tends to create an aggregated angular direction of somewhere between -60° and 60°. Over an acceptably long-time horizon -45° to 45° tends to be the most commonly observed range (anything over that tends not to be sustainable).

[170]

ii. Determinism in factors affecting price

As can be seen, reversibility and determinism are widely applicable to the macroscopic world. I will not endeavor to list all of the areas in which it is beneficial, but I would mention in passing, that underlying price data (hard or soft) can typically be understood using the laws of classical mechanics.

c. Acceleration

As noted above, it is important to be aware of acceleration when calculating a future position, because any changes in velocity can adjust the final position. That is to say any change in angular direction or speed (which together make up velocity) will alter the course of the rigid body relative to the fix and therefore such body's final position. As a result, it is important to track changes in acceleration when wayfinding or "dead-reckoning". Mathematically, acceleration (i.e. changes in velocity) will

---

[170] www.tradingview.com

change the "slope" of the "trendline" setting a new course of probability for price to travel over a given elapsed time.[171]

On a graph of price, changes in acceleration can be visualized by charting a series of linear regression or trend lines over a set time intervals. Graphically, this will evidence visually acceleration and deacceleration (since a new slope will be charted in the new time interval).

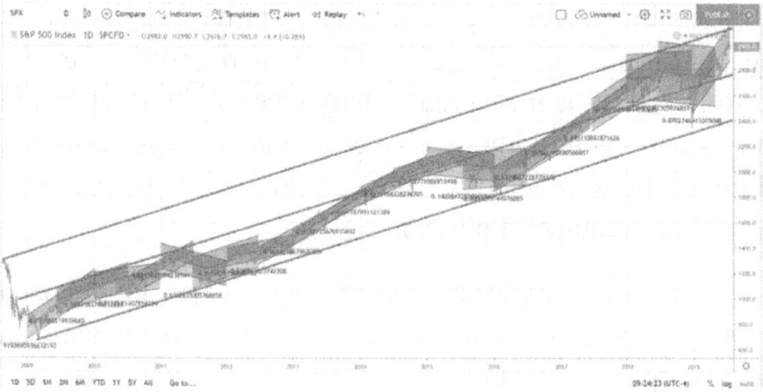
[172]

4) Fractals

Most natural occurring phenomena are actually events which are composed of the same or similar occurring component events. Said another way, most naturally occurring things are built up of component parts which resemble the whole. For instance, a tree is made up

[171] This is analogous to changing velocity in the course of one's travel in an automobile. Increasing scalar velocity will cause you to travel a distance over a shorter elapsed time, while decreasing scalar velocity will cause you to travel such distance over a longer elapsed time. In this way, price can be conceptualized (and graphically represented) the same way speed might be graphed as a function of time, charting when someone presses on the accelerator or hits the break.

[172] www.tradingview.com

of leaves, which are attached to branches, which are attached to the trunk, which makes up the tree.[173] A system, of component parts, which resemble those component parts is known as a "fractal" in science.[174]

In general terms, our previous discussion of position, velocity and acceleration is a fractal.[175] Position is a result of displacement over time, which is measured by velocity, which is measured by acceleration. Said another way, position is a result of aggregate displacement, which is measured by velocity. Velocity is in turn composed of the aggregation of all acceleration that occurred over the period velocity is measured. Many changes in acceleration can occur even without changing the average velocity. Many changes in velocity can occur even without changing the ultimate course of position.

As an example, if I am driving my car, I can speed up and slow down many times, but still end up with an average speed of 40mph. Sometimes I may travel 60mph, sometimes I may slow down to 10mph, but over the course of the entire journey my average speed might calculate out to 40mph. If you looked at my travel while I was traveling at 60mph, you might have a very different estimate of my ultimate position over a set time interval, then if you noticed immediately after my 60mph speed, I began to slow down to 10mph.

---

[173] Trees actually have an elaborate root system as well, which is similar in structure to the leaf-branch paradigm.

[174] Fractals are actually a more precise phenomenon than the one I am describing, but conceptually, our gross generalization of "self-similarity" is helpful for understanding.

[175] To some extent, all differential equations are.

In the context of price, many "trends" (or velocities) can occur within one larger trend (the average velocity), just like in the example of my car. In fact, and more accurately, these smaller trends (or smaller velocity of price) build to form a longer larger trend (or velocity over short time intervals aggregate together to give the velocity over the longer time interval).

As such, one can gain considerable information from being able to navigate between time periods, to see if there are changes in velocity occurring on a smaller scale that are likely to impact the larger trend. Or said another way, it is helpful to know if acceleration is changing in a shorter-term horizon, to determine if the expected average velocity is likely to change in a longer-time horizon.[176]

Conversely, if one is fairly confident in the certainty of the long-term destination, one might be able to determine if one thinks a change in acceleration is likely to occur over a shorter time horizon, or if a shorter time horizon's velocity is unlikely to be maintained, because of the certainty of the expectation of the average velocity and the certainty of the destination to which one is traveling.

Using my car example, once again, if you know that I am traveling to my grandma's house which is located a certain distance from me and that I desire to arrive at my grandma's house in time for a holiday dinner, if my car temporarily slows down, you might quite reasonably

---

[176] We have in fact, encountered this idea before in our discussion of the "rate of change of GDP". That is to say, it is common for individuals to look for changes in acceleration of GDP (or changes in the rate of change of GDP) to determine if forecasted velocity for GDP is likely to change (and drive into a negative period of growth or "recession").

expect, that this velocity cannot be maintained and that I am most likely to increase velocity by accelerating (and perhaps even maintain a higher than average velocity for a time, to "make up" for time lost while going slow).

In terms of price, this understanding of velocity means that trends can be tracked over many different time intervals. If a short-term trend (or velocity) is out of sync with a long-term trend (or velocity), that I am fairly certain of, I can be fairly confident in my expectation, that the short-term trend is unlikely to be sustained and that acceleration is likely to change, such that it realigns with the longer-term trend (just as in my car example).

Additionally, there are certain velocities at which, I can be fairly confident will not be maintained, because they represent an extreme velocity relative to the rigid body which is traveling.

In my car example, my car has a top speed of roughly 130mph. If I were to track my car speed on an Euclidian plane and I saw such car speed charted at roughly 130mph, I could be fairly certain in my approximation that such speed would be unlikely to be maintained over a long-period (because it is well above any reasonable speed limit and is difficult for the car to maintain without breaking based on its intrinsic design or value).

Similarly, in the context of price, there are certain velocities of price which are difficult to maintain relative to time. As an example, it is nearly impossible to maintain a velocity of 90°, since mathematically this would require the position of price to increase with such magnitude that it completely negates the constant perpetual force of time.

In sum, because position is a fractal, price is a fractal, and all markets composed of assets which have a price are also fractals. An understanding of fractals combined with an understanding of the laws of classical mechanics can be applied over different time intervals (using different strategies, but typically most similar to wayfinding) to make determinations. In the context of "technical trading", traders can use this understanding to make various trading decisions over a variety of time intervals.

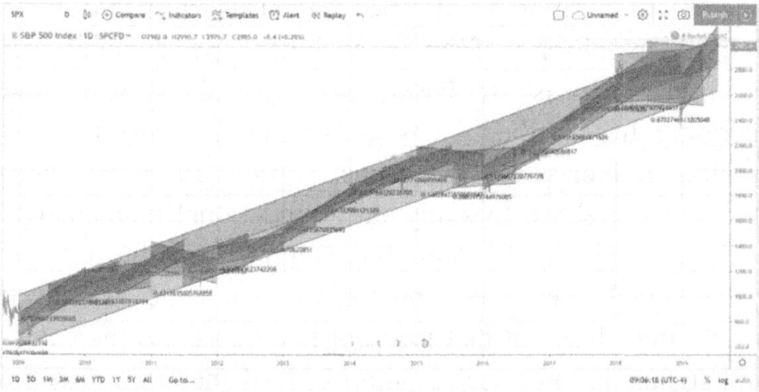
[177]

5) Other Technical Theory Rooted in Newtonian Law

We have spent a fair bit of discussion measuring the forces that effect price and how those observations and measurements can be useful in classical mechanics terms, however it is important to note that over time, individuals have developed many different strategies for making decisions based on "technical analysis" of price. We have focused on classical mechanics, because it is rooted in natural law and therefore (in my opinion), the purest

---

177 www.tradingview.com

understanding of observations on the movement of rigid bodies in the macroscopic world.

However, I would be remiss if I didn't at least mention a few of the paradigms individuals have developed to use the information measured in the preceding chapters. I would just mention, that in my view, the purest and most useful "technical analysis" of price, is necessarily the laws of classical mechanics.[178]

That is to say, just as all factors (even unknown factors) are factored into price (and is therefore most helpful to observe from a technical perspective), all technical analysis are based on "price movement" and therefore has as their basis a foundation in the laws of motion and classical mechanics. As such, it probably makes more sense to study the foundational mathematics (at least in my view), although the number of indicators and price signals that have developed over time is indeed staggering. It is not that I do not feel that these indicators and signals are not useful (almost all of them are in some way). It is that, in my general view, they are all necessarily determined based on the mathematics of classical mechanics (so an understanding of classical mechanics is probably superior in that regard than any particular indicator).

a. Leading v. Lagging Indicators

As an initial matter, it should be noted that there are two main types of indicators: "leading" and "lagging" indicators. Generally speaking, a leading indicator is a

[178] Since mathematics, is for its part, the language of nature, largely empirical, and devoid of unnecessary human interpretation and subjective input.

measurement that is believed to be predictive or indicative of a future event and a lagging indicator is a measurement of output or an event that has already occurred. This distinction is important to understand, because many people, who lack this understanding, erroneously make trading and investment decisions on the basis that certain "lagging" indicators provide predicative value which they in fact do not.[179] Therefore, it is important to understand

---

[179] This is an extraordinarily common occurrence, particularly in financial news media.

As an example, a "moving average crossover" is a lagging indicator, because it is a recordation of a certain price move that has already occurred. However, members of the financial news media continuously report these events as "golden crosses" or "death crosses" suggesting that they have predictive ability to show that price movement will continue down or continue up, based on this crossover. To be sure, the measurement itself has no predictive capability, it is predictive only to the extent that traders tend to use moving average crossovers as "confirmation" that a trend has formed and is likely to continue (i.e. that velocity is pointed in a direction and is unlikely to change) and tend to exacerbate the price movement that has already occurred. That is to say, it only has predictive value to the extent people base decisions on it with the belief it has predictive value (a form of mimeticism to be sure).

As another example, "employment numbers" (the nominal amount of individuals who are employed to those who are not) is typically used as a reference to determine whether or not an economy is performing well or poorly (that is to say, an economy is generally more productive or growing when the majority of its citizens are employed and working productively – the exception to this of course being a society where technology is so advanced production can increase without corresponding production from additional workers which is a possibility with future artificial intelligence). However, "employment numbers" are a lagging indicator because they are a recordation of a certain rate of joblessness in a prior period of time. Additionally, employment metrics are lagging by nature because mass lay-offs and firings tend to occur after earnings have begun suffering, since businesses tend not to be in the habit of firing workers in

average price generally represents where the actual price belongs (or said another way the moving average spreads out any fluctuations in price to give a "true price", which for the fundamentalist is typically compared to some value metric). As a result, people often believe in a concept of "reversion to the mean" or said another way, there is a general belief that price tends to generally stay in some accordance with its "true" or "average price", although it may temporarily stray from such price.

To be clear, mathematically, this is not entirely accurate. While price can revert such that it occupies a position closer to its average price, average price (sine it is a "moving average") can also move toward its price. That is to say, if a price deviates greatly from its moving average and stays elevated away from this moving average; provided, price doesn't move substantially, over time the moving average will rise (as new price data points are included in the moving average calculation) until it reaches a level closer to the nominal price.[182] Generally speaking,

---

actually reflect two different measurements of the same underlying position data. In the case of the trend-line or linear regression it is a measurement of velocity of such price data and therefore a leading indicator (when used in conjunction with wayfinding). In the case of the moving average or Bollinger Band it is a measurement of average price over a time interval and is therefore a measurement of prior price position or average position within a statistical range.

[182] This separates charting moving averages of price relative to price from charting price to value as discussed earlier. Since value is independent from price, it will not rise to meet price if price increases for a reason other than an increase in value (such as additional debt, speculation, etc.). Conversely, because value is a significant factor in determining price (or said mathematically price is a dependent variable of the independent variable of value) if value rises price will increase and if value falls price will tend to decrease. Additionally, because the "equilibrium price" of most assets should be somewhere

however, price reversion to its "mean" is a fairly common occurrence that people track and use for decision making with some success.

b. Pattern Trading and "Support/Resistance Levels"

Some individuals, recognizing that all factors which affect price (even potentially unknown factors known only to insiders) look solely at price for conducting "technical analysis". To do this, these individuals look for "patterns" or recurring price movements, which these individuals believe to forecast future price movement. Others characterize price in terms of level of "support" or "resistance", based on where price has been in the past and stalled (either did not surpass the level up or did not surpass the level down). This book will not concern itself with the numerous forms of pattern trading that exist.

---

near their true intrinsic value, and all productive assets operating in the physical world have a life-cycle, price will typically revert to its underlying intrinsic value during a period of decay. Thus, moving averages, typically serve as a proxy (albeit a somewhat poor one) for the principle that overtime price will tend to revert to its underlying value (typically during a decay phase in its lifecycle). To be sure however, because a moving average is a mathematical representation of a collection of data points, the moving average can rise to meet the underlying data or the price can move to revert to the mean. I will admit, however, that generally speaking, price does tend to revert to its average price, largely in my view because people believe the average price to represent true price because of its smoothing function (although this is fairly speculative and not necessarily true), the average price moves slower than price (since it is lagging price movement by the average of prior data) and the average price tends to track underlying value better (because of its smoothing functions) than any day-to-day fluctuation in price might.

It is worth mentioning, however, that almost all pattern trading is really based in kinematics (or perhaps more accurately represent a misapplication of kinematics). That is to say, many "patterns" that pattern traders rely on, would be more accurately and could be more consistently relied upon, by looking to the underlying mathematics than by relying on the pattern.

As an example, in pattern trading there is a widely relied upon price pattern known as the "double top" or "triple top". Generally speaking, a double top occurs when price hits a price, retreats from said price for a period and then increases back up to that same price it hit previously and retreats again. In a triple top, this same process occurs, except it happens three times rather than two. Others characterize this event, as price being unable to "push through resistance". Others combine, the double or triple top pattern, with other price movement to describe such movement as a "head and shoulders top".

However, if we step back from the pattern of price and look back to kinematics (rooted in foundational physics), we would deduce that a "double top" or "triple top", is more likely a situation in which velocity is approaching zero (that is to say the slope of the trend line is zero or flat). In such a situation, we might realize that the velocity of price is stagnant. Recognizing price is stagnant, we might deduce that by looking at underlying acceleration, price could either accelerate up into an up-trend or down-into a down-trend.

Said another way, the pattern of a "double top" or "triple top" and the price point of "resistance" is only relevant to the extent that it is dictated or otherwise represents the underlying kinematics.

Understanding kinematics, tends to be more accurate and consistent, because it removes the subjectiveness of "identifying a pattern" by eye or drawing arbitrary pictures on a graph, for the objectiveness of calculable vectors.

Because of the inherent subjectiveness (and relative ease), however, of identifying patterns, they can be seductive. That is to say, if you recognize a pattern and it results in a successful trade, one might be inclined to trade the same way the next time such pattern is seen (which may or may not result in success). Additionally, because pattern trades do have some basis (albeit a fairly arbitrary one) in underlying velocity, a highly observant individual might be fairly successful pattern trading (although they may be ignorant of the underlying math and why they are actually having success). The danger of course, is that it is completely, arbitrary. There is no reason for instance why a "resistance line" cannot be broken on any given day by a sufficient volume of buyers. Similarly, there is no objective reason a "double top" can't be broken through and price accelerate higher. The pattern has only an arbitrary function of exhibiting underlying physics to the extent such underlying math is consistent with such pattern.

Pattern trading tends to be a "50% of the time it works every time" mentality. The understanding of the underlying math is limited, the belief is strong, and the trading result is inconsistent.

Additionally, because of the obvious subjectivity, the danger of the nefarious alchemist is quite high. That is to say, it is fairly easy to fall victim to the magic potion, if one doesn't understand the underlying chemistry. To be clear, there are no magic patterns, just patterns which may or may not present themselves as manifestations of underling price acceleration.

1. Elliott Waves

The rare exception to the alchemy warned of above, is the "Elliott Wave". To be clear, Elliott Waves are a form of pattern recognition, but they are based on an understanding of social principles and an understanding that markets are fractals. The Elliott wave principle was created by Ralph Nelson Elliott (an accountant by profession), who recognized that markets are fractals and underlying social principles cause price fluctuations.[183]

Elliott hypothesized that crowd psychology, fluctuates naturally between optimism and pessimism. These fluctuations exhibit themselves in price (which we know is largely subjective), by creating price movements at every time interval, which build up into larger exhibitions of social mood swings.

Elliott identified that in financial markets price exhibits phases of movement. That is to say, movement in price tends to be followed by a corrective movement in the opposite direction, but of less magnitude, which builds to form a larger overall trend, which is itself subject to movement and correct movement waves or phases. In a rising economy the dominant trend is upward, whereas in a declining market the dominant trend is down. Elliott (and disciples of his who followed afterwards) created analytical

[183] Mainly growth-cycles and mimetic cycles although he characterizes them differently (mainly in terms of social mood). Elliott believed that the natural law causes humans to be subject to a rhythmical procedure, which could be observed, analyzed and calculated.

tools to identify these waves in social mood and to making trading decisions based on this recognition.[184]

Unlike Elliott, however, I find the underlying dynamic forces which result in price movement, tend to be less important for trading, than being able to analyze the movement of these forces mathematically using kinematics. That is to say, that I personally prefer kinematics because of the objectivity that can be drawn from the mathematics rather than relying on my own ability to subjectively recognize and properly labeled phases or waves, although I do not contest Elliott's underlying observations and understanding of natural law which form the basis of his theory.[185]

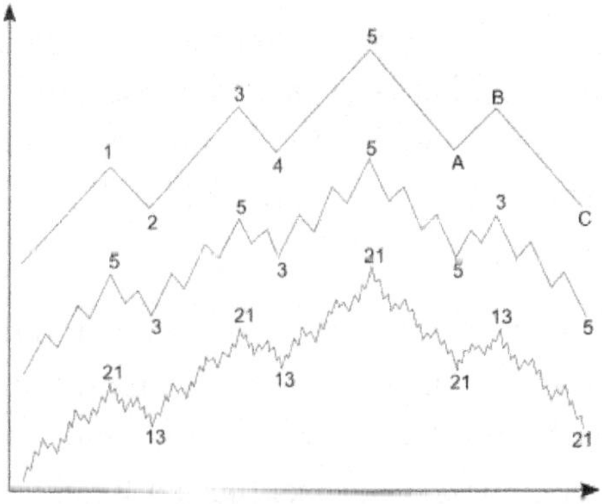

[186]

---

[184] Robert Prechter, whose book, "The Socioeconomic Theory of Finance" was mentioned in an earlier footnote was in fact one of these disciples and is highly successful Elliott Wave trader.

[185] I would note that even for the talented Elliot Wave trader, it is not uncommon to sometimes mis-characterize or identify a wave and need to correct such analysis after some movement in price has served a confirmatory function.

[186] https://en.wikipedia.org/wiki/Elliott_wave_principle#/media/File:Elliott_wave.svg

6) Non-Newtonian physics and Domain Validity

Assuming you as the reader have become convinced of the value of physics in analyzing price movements, you might begin to wonder why this book has been restricted to physical properties observed in the 17th century.

To be sure, the science of physics has made incredible advances since the 17th century. The most dramatic of which is probably the understanding of "quantum mechanics" which, generally speaking, describes nature at the smallest particle and energy levels. However, in the area of physics, the size of particles and the force of energy which cause displacement of such particles are highly relevant in making accurate calculations and approximations. In physics terms, this is known as "domain validity". That is to say, the speed and distance of particle movement is understood and approximated most accurately using equations created within a field of understanding.

In physics, macroscopic particles moving at low speed are described using classical mechanics, macroscopic particles moving at high speed are understood using relativistic mechanics, microscopic particles traveling at low speed are understood using quantum mechanics, and microscopic particles moving at high speed are understood using quantum field theory.[187] Thus, for the purpose of price, the speed is slow enough and the size large enough that its movement is best analyzed by the classical mechanics first described so long ago.

---

[187] For purposes of this discussion, macroscopic means particles larger than 10^{-9}m or nanometer and microscopic means particles smaller than a nanometer and low speed means velocity lower than 10^8 m/s and high speed means velocity greater than 10^8 m/s.

To be sure, however, some areas of quantum mechanics and relativistic mechanics have found their way into the financial world for various uses. This book will not endeavor to explain these areas other than to say other fields of physics do have utility for measuring and understanding the financial world.[188]

7) Historical Comparisons

Before we move on to the next chapter, it is important to note, that many individuals also make decisions about future decisions based on prior decisions.

That is to say, even the fundamentalist (who denies doing any technical analysis at all) will consider the historic rate of return received to determine if a current return is attractive. Many technical traders, will look to past price data, to determine if price seems "stretched" or is likely to continue higher.

To be sure, historical performance is no guarantee of future performance, however, historical data does tend to provide some insight as to future behavior because of the cyclical life-cycles (and thereby the cyclical nature) of markets. That is to say, as an example, looking back to Chapter 12, it is probably a fair assessment to say that the

---

188 Most notably, Brownian motion or "random walks" have found widespread use for modeling "stress events" for assets in a given portfolio, as they allow a computer to generate numerous potential stress events, which can then be aggregated into an "average" base case (across some standard distribution or statistical analysis) and used to prepare and make investment or banking decisions based on the potentialities which could befall any given portfolio. Similarly, high-speed trading often makes use of quantum mechanics and relativistic mechanics because of the speed at which information is processed and the speed of the trading itself.

overall public equity market is "over-valued" when the Wilshire 500 index to GDP ratio is greater than 100% (although the Wilshire 500 index to GDP ratio being 100% or greater does not necessarily predict that a market decline or end of growth-cycle is imminent).[189]

If you are not mathematically inclined, don't fret over this chapter, you can quite successfully and happily spend your life investing using the law of averaging, indexing and the barbell structure to compound with time.[190]

If you are mathematically inclined, however, you probably can already recognize the power of what has been explained. Mathematically, probabilistic price movements can be predicted and such price expectations can be used for either investing (to purchase investments cheaply thereby increasing your rate of return) or to trade price (to acquire the spread of price appreciation resulting from short-term increases in price).

I will admit that the idea of "technical analysis" at first may seem foreign, but, in truth, most people are engaged in some sort of technical analysis at all times and do not realize it. As an example, many individuals who

---

[189] It is also fairly easily recognized from viewing historical data, that overall market declines (i.e. recessions) tend to result in an approximately 50% reduction in asset price relative to the market high; which accurately reflects the reversion to value exhibited in the Wilshire 500 index to GDP ratio being overvalued at a ratio value of 1.0 or said differently when price is double value, the decline could reasonably be expected historically to result in a 50% loss in value to reduce the price back to its intrinsic value.

[190] Additionally, because your costs will be low and you enjoy exponential growth with time, it is fairly likely you will outperform your friends who like to trade, assuming they are not terribly good traders or terribly disciplined.

believe themselves to be "value investors" are in fact traders because they do no underlying analysis of value, but rather purchase assets with the general expectation that the U.S. economy tends to grow with time. Making such a determination is really a long-term "trade" (because the investor is only looking at price and not underlying value and therefore not "value investing" or "investing" at all), based on the belief that the average velocity of the U.S. economy (because of the U.S. economies inherent structure) is positive over a long-time duration.

The simple fact is, math is the law of nature and as such the law of the markets. Denying the existence of that law is akin to believing the Earth is flat or the center of the universe.

Chapter 19: Fundamental v. Technical Trading

By now it should be clear that trading can be performed on a "fundamental" or a "technical" basis.[191] Before this book concludes, it is worth noting a few potentially interesting observations.

First, fundamentalists, generally speaking, tend to enter positions early and leave trades before they are "complete". That is to say, fundamentalists tend to recognize that price doesn't accurately reflect the underlying factors that should be aggregated into the "fair price" before others tend to realize. When they do so, they tend to enter a trade thinking they will profit from when others recognize what they know to be true by pocketing this ultimate "inevitable" change in price. However, because of the nature of humankind, despite the fact there is a latent danger in price, this fact is often ignored by the market. At such point, the fundamentalist trader tends to endure a small loss (because time has transpired and they haven't received any gain and/or price may actually continue on a path in contravention of the underlying factors). As an example, it is extremely common to hear stories from experienced traders about how they knew a company should be bankrupt or was a ponzi scheme, but they went broke in the trade before the charade ultimately collapsed (often they will describe this as having had to

[191] For the particularly physics minded, one might consider the fundamentalist a trader who analyses the "dynamics" of the forces affecting price and the technical trader, a trader who analyzes and measures the kinematics exhibited by price. Although, this is an over-generalization on both accounts, depending on the nature of the trading in which a trader is engaged.

learn that their job is to make money rather than to simply be "right").[192] There is often a lag between the fundamental truth and the general markets recognition of that truth (as there is with most collective human thought).

As an example of this type of behavior, it is a fairly common experience for someone to stub their toe, wait for it to get better (even though they are aware of the underlying pain), continue to walk around on the toe (making the condition of the toe worse), before going to the doctor and finding out that their toe is now broken. At least a part of the human condition and ability to survive is based on ignoring something bad with the hopes we will survive it without consequence.

Additionally, fundamentalists tend to leave positions before the price movement in their favor is completed typically because of some set gain they have calculated they should expect to make and because they do not want to be subjected to price fluctuations which may erode their gains if they wait too long to sell.

Conversely, technical traders, tend to enter positions slightly late and they tend to leave positions a bit late. The

---

[192] I would also note that "being right" on a fundamental basis, for the trader is of little use if the market continues to be "wrong". In other words, you are only financially "right" in trading if you make money, since making money through price appreciation is the sole goal, regardless of whether your underlying analysis of financial health or sustainability is otherwise objectively "true". As such, the fundamental trader can frequently find them self in a quixotic mindset, where they hold a belief vehemently, even though everyone else has dispensed with the idealism of the underlying facts and are rather enjoying the (typically debt laden) ride of prices to "prosperity" without regard for the true health or sustainability of the underlying financial or economic conditions.

reason for this is that most technical trading models require some form of "trend" or "price" confirmation. That is to say, it is safer to enter a position, after at least a portion of the market has recognized that something is wrong, than it is to enter it while everyone thinks things are great (because you don't start out in a loss position and relying on price confirming direction is generally more accurate than "predicting" or "guessing" a direction). Missing the beginning (or first wave or phase) of a trade tends not to overly concern technical traders, because they looking to capture the bulk of the main price movement along a trend (and would rather avoid the temporary misfortune of an upfront loss in any case). Similarly, technical traders tend to remain in a trade, until a trade or trend has been "broken". That is to say, when the price has reversed course from the expected direction. Such a "break" tends to confirm that the "price action" is over and that the trade should be closed. As such, a small loss in overall gains tends to be suffered at the end of the trade.[193]

---

[193] Some technical traders, view this as a superior model, because the loss comes out of gains rather than principal upfront. The logic of this is not unlike the house in blackjack, where it is generally statistically better, to give someone else the opportunity to bust upfront and to be in the position of not needing to look at your cards to see if you have busted until you have already received at least some gains. There also tends to be less psychological and emotional impact from losing a portion of gains than losing a portion of principal prior to receiving gains since one doesn't begin in a "net loss" position. Said another way, fundamental traders often feel the need to explain why they are right even when superficially it does not appear so and tend to be someone emotionally taxed as a result, while technical traders tend to just flow with wherever the river of price is headed.

To be sure an understanding of both and the inherent risks of each are important to becoming a successful trader.

Conclusion

As with most things in life, the most important thing (even if you don't fully understand) is just to get started (you will inevitably learn with experience if you just try at the beginning). Additionally, for the purposes of investing, the more time you have (and the bigger the lump sum you have to start with at the beginning) the better off you are (although your strategy will play a large role in your success). That is to say, time inevitably is a factor with which we all have to deal. It is in fact the most precious resource of any living creature. All aspects of life are dragged along at that continuous and perpetual horizontal vector toward the future. This makes life very beautiful, in that moments become precious to us, but in terms of your finances time is money. The more time you have to invest the better the returns you can enjoy (again when done correctly), so it is best to get started as soon as possible. If you can't do anything else you can index and law of average, until you figure out what you would like to do. If you are a parent, you should start investing for your children so they have a leg up when they come of age.

It should also be noted that over a long-time horizon life is cyclical. That is to say, the same forces and tensions experienced by humans in years past tend to arise in the future. The same economic struggles emerge between countries and businesses as they jostle for power. The same political struggles emerge between populations and their governments. The same ideological struggles emerge between different political bodies. The players change, but the game remains the same.

With that said, relative to the human life span, the long-term market cycle, generally speaking, exceeds the expected life span of most humans. That is to say, if you look back at the cycle for the "risk-free" rate of return is approximately 40-80 years. Because the risk-free rate is the rate of return on which all assets are based, in general, long-term market cycles (and long-term debt cycles) tend to last for 40-80 years.

During times when the risk free-rate is high and the market is undervalued (these two events being likely to co-exist since the risk-free rate will deprioritize purchasing equities because of their relative greater risk on the risk continuum), an individual will likely benefit from being a net purchaser of the risk-free rate and from being a purchaser of equities on a long-term basis (that is to say, over the next 40-80 years).[194] During times when the risk-free rate is low and the market is overvalued (these events being likely to co-exist since the risk-free rate will prioritize the purchasing of equities because of their relative greater return), an individual will likely benefit from being a net seller of equities.[195] Thus, being able to recognize long-term market cycles will likely serve that individual well compared to a similarly individual who is unable to recognize the opportunities they present. That is to say "the successful [person] is the one who had the chance and took it".[196] Given the length of the average

---

[194] Although over a short-term or medium-term such decision making may not seem as attractive.

[195] During times where the equity market is overvalued and risk free rate is high, it would make sense to purchase the risk free rate. During times where the equity market is undervalued and the risk-free rate is low, it would make sense to purchase the equity market. However, I would mention that neither of these situations should be likely to occur, given the risk of the equity market would be decoupled from the risk of the risk-free rate.

[196] Attributed to Roger Babson.

human life (approximately 75 years) and the average length of the long-term financial cycles (of approximately 40-80 years), it is unlikely an individual will experience more than one of these circumstances in their lifetime in any event, so they may very well represent once in a lifetime opportunities.[197]

Over the medium term, market cycles will be subject to growth and decay phases (termed "expansions" and "recessions"). Expansions will tend to last 10 years for every three years of recession. Once again, the ability to observe these cycles, should create opportunities for relatively cheap purchasing or relativity over-valued selling, given the ability of the individual to recognize events as such (and avoid the mimetic process that comes around with them).

Over the short-term, the talented trader may be able to make use of kinematics and fundamentals to profit from short-term fluctuations of price (between years, quarters, months, weeks or even days).

---

[197] It is likely, however, that during these cycles, individuals will begin to postulate that there is a "new normal" and that this is how things will be forever. During a time of overvaluation for instance, people may claim that value investing is dead and will never be the same. You can be assured that it is not, it is simply a function of the fact that during times of low interest rates, asset prices tend to get overvalued relative to GDP, but still look attractive relative to the risk-free rate. At such point, value investing will seem to provide inferior returns to "growth investing" because it won't benefit from the price appreciation being enjoyed by the fact everything is overvalued. Despite the fact markets are cyclical, people will look to this as proof value investing "doesn't work anymore". To be sure, it does and will work in the future, it is just temporarily disincentivized by the long-term market cycle.

Regardless of strategy or timing however, the fundamentals are the same. There is a difference between price and value. The difference can be determined using metrics of price and comparing those to metrics of value.

There is a continuum of risk (across the capital structure) for any asset that can be purchased (that is the risk of loss of principal and the loss of expected future returns). Generally speaking, return is a function of the relative risk of any asset or one's position in the capital structure (based on a premium calculated relative to the risk-free rate of return). Mathematically, one will benefit by focusing investment on either end of the risk-continuum, because risk-adjusted return improves at each extreme end of the capital structure (i.e. the "barbell" strategy).

Investing is an analysis of value relative to the price paid. Investing enjoys the compounding benefit of cashflow receipts over time. If you are just looking at price, regardless of the time horizon, you are not investing, you are trading.

Trading is an analysis solely of price and/or the factors which make up the forces which cause it to move. Trading can be evaluated based on an understanding of those underlying forces or by measuring the displacement of those forces. Each strategy has inherent strengths and weakness, but both are certainly possible within the context of certain markets and time frames (although many, perhaps even most, lack the discipline and precision to do so effectively). All price movement is subject to the laws of classical mechanics and can be understood in those terms.

If all else fails, averaging price, keeping costs low, indexing, a time horizon that maximizes compounding and "barbell-style" asset selection will serve just fine to increase wealth.

If you have personal debt, the best thing you can do is pay it off and get rid of it. Debt has the benefit of compounding interest with time. As a personal debtor, you are the source of investment for someone else, or said another way, the expense of the money you borrowed compounds with time to reduce the amount of money you have and increase the amount of money the lender has.

Using leverage for productive assets improves purchasing power at a low cost of capital and therefore increases return. Beware of over-leveraging and the asymmetry of risk, at the expense of losing more than you stand to gain (as well as losing the benefits of compounding).

In the end the most important asset is time. It is an absolute force which none of us can escape. There is no asset more important than having the freedom to do what you want with the people you want with the time that you have. Do not be afraid to try. Neither success or failure is ever really permanent and the two most important factors of success are getting started and never quitting. Even if you fail, there is no price that can be placed on character and experience. "Property may be destroyed and money may lose its purchasing power; but character, health, knowledge and good judgment will always be in demand under all circumstances."[198]

[198] Attributed to Roger Babson.

I hope this book will enrich both your financial and your personal life and that you will live the life you intend with the time you are given.

With tremendous gratitude to the reader,

- Will DeCotiis.

Made in United States
Orlando, FL
04 November 2026

90207804R00174